RITE OF
CHRISTIAN INITIATION
OF ADULTS

THE ROMAN RITUAL

REVISED BY DECREE OF THE
SECOND VATICAN ECUMENICAL
COUNCIL AND PUBLISHED BY
AUTHORITY OF POPE PAUL VI

BURNS & OATES
A Continuum imprint
LONDON • NEW YORK

VERITAS
PUBLICATIONS
DUBLIN

RITE OF CHRISTIAN INITIATION OF ADULTS

**APPROVED FOR USE IN THE DIOCESES OF
ENGLAND AND WALES, IRELAND, AND SCOTLAND**

Prepared by
International Commission on English in the Liturgy
A Joint Commission of Catholic Bishops' Conferences

BURNS & OATES
A Continuum imprint
The Tower Building, 11 York Road,
London, SE1 7NX

VERITAS PUBLICATIONS
7–8 Lower Abbey Street
Dublin 1

Reprinted 2004

ISBN 0 86012 3723 (hardback)
ISBN 0 86012 3731 (paperback)

ACKNOWLEDGEMENTS

The English translation, original texts, additional notes, arrangements, and design of *Rite of Christian Initiation of Adults* © 1985, International Committee on English in the Liturgy, Inc. (ICEL); excerpts from the English translation of *The Roman Missal* © 1973, ICEL; excerpts from *Pastoral Care of the Sick: Rites of Anointing and Viaticum* © 1982, ICEL. All rights reserved. The texts of the Gospel readings used in Appendix 3 of this volume are taken from *The Jerusalem Bible* © 1966 Darton, Longman & Todd, Ltd. Used with permission.

Printed in the United Kingdom by Henry Ling Limited, at the Dorset Press, Dorchester, DT1 1HD

CONTENTS

PART II: RITES FOR PARTICULAR CIRCUMSTANCES

EDITORIAL NOTE

The *Rite of Christian Initiation of Adults* is the ICEL translation of the 1974 emended second printing of the *Ordo initiationis christianae adultorum*. Because this second printing contained the *Praenotanda de initiatione christiana*, a translation of this is included in this English edition and is entitled 'Christian Initiation, General Introduction.' This document has its own self-contained enumeration of paragraphs, to which there are several cross-references in the *Rite of Christian Initiation of Adults*. The present ICEL edition incorporates the emendations of the text necessitated by the Code of Canon Law of 1983 and issued by the Congregation for Divine Worship on 12 September 1983.

This White Book text of the *Rite of Christian Initiation of Adults* replaces the interim or Green Book text issued by ICEL in 1974.

The main body of the text of the present edition begins with the Introduction proper to the *Rite of Christian Initiation of Adults*. In the interest of pastoral utility and convenience, the English edition somewhat rearranges the contents of the *praenotanda* of the Latin *editio typica*. The Introduction moves directly from the section entitled 'Structure of the Initiation of Adults,' which presents a general outline of the steps and periods of the process of Christian initiation, to the section entitled 'Ministries and Offices.' The paragraphs in the Latin *editio typica* (nos. 9-40) devoted to a detailed description of each of the steps and periods of the entire catechumenate have been integrated with the correlative paragraphs of the particular introductions to each of those steps and periods, so that all relevant material is concentrated in its place of application. In the section entitled 'Structure of the Initiation of Adults,' cross-references are given to these particular introductions. This editorial rearrangement omits nothing from the Latin original, but it does entail a departure from the paragraph enumeration of the Latin edition. For each paragraph of the English edition bearing the number proper to this edition, the right-hand margin carries the reference number or numbers indicating the corresponding paragraph or paragraphs of the Latin edition. A reference number in the right-hand margin that is preceded by a letter indicates a text from a source other than the *Ordo initiationis christianae adultorum*; numbers that are preceded by the letters 'PC' refer to *Pastoral Care of the Sick: Rites of Anointing and Viaticum*; numbers preceded by 'R' refer to the appendix of the *Ordo initiationis*, 'Rite of Reception of Baptised Christians into the Full Communion of the Catholic Church.'

After the introduction to the *Rite of Christian Initiation of Adults*, the new English edition of this ritual presents the contents in two parts.

Part I, entitled 'Christian Initiation of Adults,' consists of the steps and periods that make up the full and paradigmatic form of Christian initiation, in accord with the restoration of the integral catechumenate decreed by the Second Vatican Council.

Part II, entitled 'Rites for Particular Circumstances', consists of material for: the adaptation of the rite to unbaptised children of catechetical age; exceptional circumstances in which the process of Christian initiation is not followed in its complete form; situations in which those already baptised are either to be catechized and complete their Christian initiation or are to become part of the full communion of the Catholic Church; and circumstances in which the rite of reception into the full communion of the Catholic Church is integrated with the celebration at the Easter Vigil of the sacraments of initiation.

Careful attention to the convenience of the minister has guided the format and presentation of each of the rites. An outline preceding each rite gives the minister a concise overview of the structure. The various options and alternatives provided within the rites are indicated simply and distinctly; introductory material, rubrics, and liturgical texts for each rite are typographically set off from each other. The full texts of the readings and psalms required for the liturgy of the word in celebrations are not printed out, since it is presumed that, in keeping with liturgical norms, they will be proclaimed from a Lectionary or Bible. Accordingly, either references to the Lectionary for Mass are given for the readings and psalms belonging to each celebration or a list of citations of suitable readings is given at the place of their occurrence in the particular rite.

CONGREGATION FOR DIVINE WORSHIP

Prot. no. 15/72

DECREE

The Second Vatican Council prescribed the revision of the rite of baptism of adults and decreed that the catechumenate for adults, divided into several steps, should be restored. By this means the time of the catechumenate, which is intended as a period of well-suited instruction, would be sanctified by liturgical rites to be celebrated at successive intervals of time. The Council likewise decreed that both the solemn and simple rites of adult baptism should be revised, with proper attention to the restored catechumenate.

In observance of these decrees, the Congregation for Divine Worship prepared a new rite for the Christian initiation of adults, which Pope Paul VI has approved. The Congregation now publishes it and declares the present edition to be the *editio typica*, to replace the rite of baptism of adults now in the Roman Ritual. It likewise decrees that this new rite may be used in Latin at once and in the vernacular from the day appointed by the conference of bishops, after it has prepared a translation and had it confirmed by the Apostolic See.

All things to the contrary notwithstanding.

From the office of the Congregation for Divine Worship, 6 January 1972, Epiphany.

Arturo Cardinal Tabera
Prefect

A. Bugnini
Secretary

EPISCOPAL CONFERENCE OF ENGLAND AND WALES
and
EPISCOPAL CONFERENCE OF SCOTLAND

After his resurrection from the dead, Jesus commanded his disciples, 'Go, therefore, make disciples of all nations; baptise them in the name of the Father and of the Son and of the Holy Spirit, and teach them to observe all the commands I gave you.' (Matthew 28:19–20)

Those words were taken to heart by the men and women of the early Church, and the teaching and initiation of converts into the Christian community, culminating in the Easter celebration of baptism, confirmation and eucharist, came to be one of the glories of the Church.

The English language text of the Rite of Christian Initiation of Adults, contained in this volume, is an important part of the Church's desire to restore the adult catechumenate to its rightful place in the life of our communities. This Rite is the exemplar and rule for all Christian Initiation and we therefore commend it to the attention of all parish communities, and direct that it be implemented by the First Sunday of Advent 1988 so replacing any previous interim versions

Confirmed by the Congregation for Divine Worship,
for England and Wales, Protocol no. 515/86, 20 June 1986;
for Scotland, Protocol no. 685/86, 18 June 1986.

EPISCOPAL CONFERENCE OF IRELAND

After his resurrection from the dead, Jesus commanded his disciples, 'Go, therefore, make disciples of all nations; baptise them in the name of the Father and of the Son and of the Holy Spirit, and teach them to observe all the commands I gave you.' (Matthew 28: 19-20)

Those words were taken to heart by the men and women of the early Church, and the teaching and initiation of converts into the Christian community, culminating in the Easter celebration of baptism, confirmation and eucharist, came to be one of the glories of the Church.

The English language text of the Rite of Christian Initiation of Adults, contained in this volume, is an important part of the Church's desire to restore the adult catechumenate to its rightful place in the life of our communities. This Rite is the exemplar and rule for all Christian Initiation and we therefore commend it to the attention of all parish communities.

Confirmed by the Congregation for Divine Worship,
for Ireland, Protocol no. 696/86, June 1986.

CHRISTIAN INITIATION, GENERAL INTRODUCTION

1 In the sacraments of Christian initiation we are freed from the power of darkness and joined to Christ's death, burial, and resurrection. We receive the Spirit of filial adoption and are part of the entire people of God in the celebration of the memorial of the Lord's death and resurrection.[1]

2 Baptism incorporates us into Christ and forms us into God's people. This first sacrament pardons all our sins, rescues us from the power of darkness, and brings us to the dignity of adopted children,[2] a new creation through water and the Holy Spirit. Hence we are called and are indeed the children of God.[3]

By signing us with the gift of the Spirit, confirmation makes us more completely the image of the Lord and fills us with the Holy Spirit, so that we may bear witness to him before all the world and work to bring the Body of Christ to its fulness as soon as possible.[4]

Finally, coming to the table of the eucharist, we eat the flesh and drink the blood of the Son of Man so that we may have eternal life[5] and show forth the unity of God's people. By offering ourselves with Christ, we share in the universal sacrifice, that is, the entire community of the redeemed offered to God by their High Priest,[6] and we pray for a greater outpouring of the Holy Spirit, so that the whole human race may be brought into the unity of God's family.[7]

Thus the three sacraments of Christian initiation closely combine to bring us, the faithful of Christ, to his full stature and to enable us to carry out the mission of the entire people of God in the Church and in the world.[8]

Dignity of Baptism

3 Baptism, the door to life and to the kingdom of God, is the first sacrament of the New Law, which Christ offered to all, that they might have eternal life.[9] He later entrusted this sacrament and the Gospel to his Church, when he told his apostles: 'Go, make disciples of all nations, and baptise them in the name of the Father, and of the Son, and of the Holy Spirit.'[10] Baptism is therefore, above all, the sacrament of that faith by which, enlightened by the grace of the Holy Spirit, we respond to the Gospel of Christ. That is why the Church believes that it is its most basic and necessary duty to inspire all, catechumens, parents of children still to be baptised, and godparents, to that true and living faith by which they hold fast to Christ and enter into or confirm their commitment to the New Covenant. In order to enliven such faith, the Church prescribes the pastoral instruction of catechumens, the preparation of the children's parents, the celebration of God's word, and the profession of faith at the celebration of baptism.

4 Further, baptism is the sacrament by which its recipients are incorporated into the Church and are built up together in the Spirit into a house where God lives,[11] into a holy nation and a royal priesthood.[12] Baptism is a sacramental bond of unity linking all who have been signed by it.[13] Because of that unchangeable effect (given ex-

---

[1] See Vatican Council II, Decree on the Church's Missionary Activity *Ad gentes*, no. 14.

[2] See Colossians 1:13; Romans 8:15; Galatians 4:5. See also Council of Trent, sess. 6., *Decr. de justificatione*, cap. 4: Denz.-Schön. 1524.

[3] See 1 John 3:1.

[4] See Vatican Council II, Decree on the Church's Missionary Activity *Ad gentes*, no. 36.

[5] See John 6:55.

[6] See Augustine, *De civitate Dei* 10,6: PL 41, 284. Vatican Council II, Dogmatic Constitution on the Church *Lumen gentium*, no. 11; Decree on the Ministry and Life of Priests *Presbyterorum Ordinis*, no. 2.

[7] See Vatican Council II, Dogmatic Constitution on the Church *Lumen gentium*, no. 28.

[8] See ibid., no. 31.

[9] See John 3:5.

[10] Matthew 28:19.

[11] See Ephesians 2:22.

[12] See 1 Peter 2:9.

[13] See Vatican Council II, Decree on Ecumenism *Unitatis redintegratio*, no. 22.

---

pression in the Latin liturgy by the anointing of the baptised person with chrism in the presence of God's people), the rite of baptism is held in highest honour by all Christians. Once it has been validly celebrated, even if by Christians with whom we are not in full communion, it may never lawfully be repeated.

5   Baptism, the cleansing with water by the power of the living word,[14] washes away every stain of sin, original and personal, makes us sharers in God's own life[15] and his adopted children.[16] As proclaimed in the prayers for the blessing of the water, baptism is a cleansing water of rebirth[17] that makes us God's children born from on high. The blessed Trinity is invoked over those who are to be baptised, so that all who are signed in this name are consecrated to the Trinity and enter into communion with the Father, the Son, and the Holy Spirit. They are prepared for this high dignity and led to it by the scriptural readings, the prayer of the community, and their own profession of belief in the Father, the Son, and the Holy Spirit.

6   Far superior to the purifications of the Old Law, baptism produces these effects by the power of the mystery of the Lord's passion and resurrection. Those who are baptised are united to Christ in a death like his;[18] buried with him in death, they are given life again with him, and with him they rise again.[19] For baptism recalls and makes present the paschal mystery itself, because in baptism we pass from the death of sin into life. The celebration of baptism should therefore reflect the joy of the resurrection, especially when the celebration takes place during the Easter Vigil or on a Sunday.

Offices and Ministries of Baptism

7   The preparation for baptism and Christian instruction are both of vital concern to God's people, the Church, which hands on and nourishes the faith received from the apostles. Through the ministry of the Church, adults are called to the Gospel by the Holy Spirit and infants are bap-

tized in the faith of the Church and brought up in that faith. Therefore it is most important that catechists and other lay-persons should work with priests and deacons in the preparation for baptism. In the actual celebration, the people of God (represented not only by the parents, godparents, and relatives, but also, as far as possible, by friends, neigbours, and some members of the local Church) should take an active part. Thus they will show their common faith and the shared joy with which the newly baptised are received into the community of the Church.

8   It is a very ancient custom of the Church that adults are not admitted to baptism without godparents, members of the Christian community who will assist the candidates at least in the final preparation for baptism and after baptism will help them persevere in the faith and in their lives as Christians. In the baptism of children, as well, godparents are to be present in order to represent both the expanded spiritual family of the one to be baptised and the role of the Church as a mother. As occasion offers, godparents help the parents so that children will come to profess the faith and live up to it.

9   At least in the later rites of the catechumenate and in the actual celebration of baptism, the part of godparents is to testify to the faith of adult candidates or, together with the parents, to profess the Church's faith, in which children are baptised.

10 Therefore godparents, chosen by the catechumens or by the families of children to be baptised, must, in the judgment of the parish priest (pastor), be qualified to carry out the proper liturgical functions mentioned in no. 9.

    1. Godparents are persons, other than
       the parents of candidates, who are designated by the candidates themselves

---

[14] See Ephesians 5:26.

[15] See 2 Peter 1:4.

[16] See Romans 8:15; Galatians 4:5.

[17] See Titus 3:5.

[18] See Romans 6:4-5.

[19] See Ephesians 2:5-6.

or by a candidate's parents or whoever stands in the place of parents, or, in the absence of these, by the parish priest (pastor) or the minister of baptism. Each candidate may have either a godmother or a godfather or both a godmother and a godfather.

2. Those designated must have the capability and intention of carrying out the responsibility of a godparent and be mature enough to do so. A person sixteen years of age is presumed to have the requisite maturity, but the diocesan bishop may have stipulated another age or the parish priest (pastor) or the minister may decide that there is a legitimate reason for allowing an exception.

3. Those designated as godparents must have received the three sacraments of initiation, baptism, confirmation, and eucharist, and be living a life consistent with faith and with the responsibility of a godparent.

4. Those designated as godparents must also be members of the Catholic Church and be canonically free to carry out this office. At the request of parents, a baptised and believing Christian not belonging to the Catholic Church may act as a Christian witness along with a Catholic godparent.[20] In the case of separated Eastern Christians with whom we do not have full communion the special discipline for the Eastern Churches is to be respected.

11 The ordinary ministers of baptism are bishops, priests, and deacons.

1. In every celebration of this sacrament they should be mindful that they act in the Church in the name of Christ and by the power of the Holy Spirit.

2. They should therefore be diligent in the ministry of the word of God and in the manner of celebrating the sacrament. They must avoid any action that the faithful could rightly regard as favouritism.[21]

3. Except in a case of necessity, these ministers are not to confer baptism outside their own territory, even on their own subjects, without the requisite permission.

12 Bishops are the chief stewards of the mysteries of God and leaders of the entire liturgical life in the Church committed to them.[22] This is why they direct the conferring of baptism, which brings to the recipient a share in the kingly priesthood of Christ.[23] Therefore bishops should personally celebrate baptism, especially at the Easter Vigil. They should have a particular concern for the preparation and baptism of adults.

13 It is the duty of parish priests (pastors) to assist the bishop in the instruction and baptism of the adults entrusted to their care, unless the bishop makes other provisions. Parish priests (pastors), with the assistance of catechists or other qualified lay-persons, have the duty of preparing the parents and godparents of children through appropriate pastoral guidance and of baptising the children.

14 Other priests and deacons, since they are co-workers in the ministry of bishops and parish priests (pastors), also prepare candidates for baptism and, by the invitation or consent of the bishop or parish priest (pastor), celebrate the sacrament.

15 The celebrant of baptism may be assisted by other priests and deacons and also by lay-persons in those parts that pertain to them, especially if there are a large number to be baptised. Provision for this is made in various parts of the rituals for adults and for children.

16 In imminent danger of death and especially at the moment of death, when no priest or deacon is available, any member of the faithful, indeed anyone with the right intention, may and sometimes must administer baptism. In a case simply of danger of death the sacrament should be

---

[20] See *Codex Iuris Canonici*, can. 873 and 874, §§ 1 and 2.

[21] See Vatican Council II, Constitution on the Liturgy *Sacrosanctum Concilium*, art. 32; Pastoral Constitution on the Church in the Modern World *Gaudium et spes*, no. 29.

[22] See Vatican Council II, Decree on the Pastoral Office of Bishops *Christus Dominus*, no. 15.

[23] See Vatican Council II, Dogmatic Constitution on the Church *Lumen gentium*, no. 26.

administered, if possible, by a member of the faithful according to one of the shorter rites provided for this situation.[24] Even in this case a small community should be formed to assist at the rite or, if possible, at least one or two witnesses should be present.

17 Since they belong to the priestly people, all lay-persons, especially parents and, by reason of their work, catechists, midwives, family or social workers or nurses of the sick, as well as physicians and surgeons, should be thoroughly aware, according to their capacities, of the proper method of baptising in case of emergency. They should be taught by parish priests (pastors), deacons, and catechists. Bishops should provide appropriate means within their diocese for such instruction.

Requirements for the Celebration of Baptism

18 The water used in baptism should be true water and, both for the sake of authentic sacramental symbolism and for hygienic reasons, should be pure and clean.

19 The baptismal font, or the vessel in which on occasion the water is prepared for celebration of the sacrament in the sanctuary, should be spotlessly clean and of pleasing design.

20 If the climate requires, provision should be made for the water to be heated beforehand.

21 Except in case of necessity, a priest or deacon is to use only water that has been blessed for the rite. The water blessed at the Easter Vigil should, if possible, be kept and used throughout the Easter season to signify more clearly the relationship between the sacrament of baptism and the paschal mystery. Outside the Easter season, it is desirable that the water be blessed for each occasion, in order that the words of blessing may explicitly express the mystery of salvation that the Church remembers and proclaims. If the baptistery is supplied with running water, the blessing is given as the water flows.

22 As the rite for baptising, either immersion, which is more suitable as a symbol of participation in the death and resurrection of Christ, or pouring may lawfully be used.

23 The words for conferring baptism in the Latin Church are: I BAPTISE YOU IN THE NAME OF THE FATHER, AND OF THE SON, AND OF THE HOLY SPIRIT.

24 For celebrating the liturgy of the word of God a suitable place should be provided in the baptistery or in the church.

25 The baptistery or the area where the baptismal font is located should be reserved for the sacrament of baptism and should be worthy to serve as the place where Christians are reborn in water and the Holy Spirit. The baptistery may be situated in a chapel either inside or outside the church or in some other part of the church easily seen by the faithful; it should be large enough to accommodate a good number of people. After the Easter season, the Easter candle should be kept reverently in the baptistery, in such a way that it can be lighted for the celebration of baptism and so that from it the candles for the newly baptised can easily be lighted.

26 In the celebration the parts of the rite that are to be celebrated outside the baptistery should be carried out in different areas of the church that most conveniently suit the size of the congregation and the several parts of the baptismal liturgy. When the baptistery cannot accommodate all the catechumens and the congregation, the parts of the rite that are customarily celebrated inside the baptistery may be transferred to some other suitable area of the church.

27 As far as possible, all recently born babies should be baptised at a common celebration on the same day. Except for a good reason, baptism should not be celebrated more than once on the same day in the same church.

28 Further details concerning the time for baptism of adults and of children will be

---

[24] See *Rite of Christian Initiation of Adults*, nos. 351-375; *Rite of Baptism for Children*, nos. 157-164.

found in the respective rituals. But at all times the celebration of the sacrament should have a markedly paschal character.

29 Parish priests (pastors) must carefully and without delay record in the baptismal register the names of those baptised, of the minister, parents, and godparents, as well as the place and date of baptism.

*Adaptations by the
Conferences of Bishops*

30 According to the Constitution on the Liturgy (art. 63, b), it is within the competence of the conferences of bishops to compose for their local rituals a section corresponding to this one in the Roman Ritual, adapted to the needs of their respective regions. After it has been reviewed by the Apostolic See, it may be used in the regions for which it was prepared.

In this connection, it is the responsibility of each conference of bishops:

1. to decide on the adaptations mentioned in the Constitution on the Liturgy (art. 39);

2. carefully and prudently to weigh what elements of a people's distinctive traditions and culture may suitably be admitted into divine worship and so to propose to the Apostolic See other adaptations considered useful or necessary that will be introduced with its consent;

3. to retain distinctive elements of any existing local rituals, as long as they conform to the Constitution on the Liturgy and correspond to contemporary needs, or to modify such elements;

4. to prepare translations of the texts that genuinely reflect the characteristics of various languages and cultures and to add, whenever helpful, music suitable for singing;

5. to adapt and augment the Introductions contained in the Roman Ritual, so that the ministers may fully understand the meaning of the rites and carry them out effectively;

6. to arrange the material in the various editions of the liturgical books prepared under the guidance of the conference of bishops, so that these books may better suit pastoral use.

31 Taking into consideration especially the norms in the Constitution on the Liturgy (art. 37-40, 65), the conferences of bishops in mission countries have the responsibility of judging whether the elements of initiation in use among some peoples can be adapted for the rite of Christian baptism and of deciding whether such elements are to be incorporated into the rite.

32 When the Roman Ritual for baptism provides several optional formularies, local rituals may add other formularies of the same kind.

33 The celebration of baptism is greatly enhanced by the use of song, which stimulates in the participants a sense of their unity, fosters their praying together, and expresses the joy of Easter that should permeate the whole rite. The conference of bishops should therefore encourage and help specialists in music to compose settings for those liturgical texts particularly suited to congregational singing.

*Adaptations by the
Minister of Baptism*

34 Taking into account existing circumstances and other needs, as well as the wishes of the faithful, the minister should make full use of the various options allowed in the rite.

35 In addition to the adaptations that are provided in the Roman Ritual for the dialogue and blessings, the minister may make other adaptations for special circumstances. These adaptations will be indicated more fully in the Introductions to the rites of baptism for adults and for children.

RITE OF CHRISTIAN INITIATION OF ADULTS

There is one Lord, one faith, one baptism,
one God, the Father of all

RITE OF CHRISTIAN INITIATION OF ADULTS

INTRODUCTION

1   The rite of Christian initiation presented here is designed for adults who, after hearing the mystery of Christ proclaimed, consciously and freely seek the living God and enter the way of faith and conversion as the Holy Spirit opens their hearts. By God's help they will be strengthened spiritually during their preparation and at the proper time will receive the sacraments fruitfully.

2   This rite includes not simply the celebration of the sacraments of baptism, confirmation, and eucharist, but also all the rites belonging to the catechumenate. Endorsed by the ancient practice of the Church, a catechumenate that would be suited to contemporary missionary activity in all regions was so widely requested that the Second Vatican Council decreed its restoration, revision, and adaptation to local traditions.[1]

3   So that the rite of initiation will be more useful for the work of the Church and for individual, parochial, and missionary circumstances, the rite is first presented in Part I of this book in its complete and usual form (nos. 36-241). This is designed for the preparation of a group of candidates, but by simple adaptation parish priests (pastors) can devise a form suited to one person.

Part II provides rites for special circumstances: the Christian initiation of children (nos. 242-306), a simple form of the rite for adults to be carried out in exceptional circumstances (nos. 307-345), and a short form of the rite for those in danger of death (nos. 346-375). Part II also includes guidelines for preparing uncatechized adults for confirmation and eucharist (nos. 376-386), the rite of reception of baptised Christians into the full communion of the Catholic Church (nos. 387-417), and a rite combining this reception with celebration of Christian initiation at the Easter Vigil (nos. 418-451).

---

[1] See Vatican Council II, Constitution on the Liturgy *Sacrosanctum Concilium*, art. 64-66; Decree on the Church's Missionary Activity *Ad gentes*, no. 14; Decree on the Pastoral Office of Bishops *Christus Dominus*, no. 14.

4   The initiation of catechumens is a gradual process that takes place   4
within the community of the faithful. By joining the catechumens in reflect-
ing on the value of the paschal mystery and by renewing their own conversion, the faithful provide an example that will help the catechumens to obey
the Holy Spirit more generously.

5   The rite of initiation is suited to a spiritual journey of adults that varies   5
according to the many forms of God's grace, the free cooperation of the
individuals, the action of the Church, and the circumstances of time and
place.

6   This journey includes not only the periods for making inquiry and   6
for maturing (see no. 7), but also the steps marking the catechumens' progress, as they pass, so to speak, through another doorway or ascend to the
next level.

   1. The first step: reaching the point of initial conversion and wishing
   to become Christians, they are accepted as catechumens by the Church.

   2. The second step: having progressed in faith and nearly completed
   the catechumenate, they are accepted into a more intense preparation for the sacraments of initiation.

   3. The third step: having completed their spiritual preparation, they
   receive the sacraments of Christian initiation.

These three steps are to be regarded as the major, more intense moments of initiation and are marked by three liturgical rites: the first by the
rite of acceptance into the order of catechumens (nos. 41-74); the second
by the rite of election or enrolment of names (nos. 105-124); and the third
by the celebration of the sacraments of Christian initiation (nos. 198-233).

7   The steps lead to periods of inquiry and growth; alternatively the peri-   7
ods may also be seen as preparing for the ensuing step.

   1. The first period consists of inquiry on the part of the candidates
   and of evangelization and the precatechumenate on the part of the
   Church. It ends with the rite of acceptance into the order of catechumens.

   2. The second period, which begins with the rite of acceptance into
   the order of catechumens and may last for several years, includes
   catechesis and the rites connected with catechesis. It comes to an end
   on the day of election.

   3. The third and much shorter period, which follows the rite of election, ordinarily coincides with the Lenten preparation for the Easter
   celebration and the sacraments of initiation. It is a time of purification and enlightenment and includes the celebration of the rites belonging to this period.

4. The final period extends through the whole Easter season and is devoted to the postbaptismal catechesis or mystagogy. It is a time for deepening the Christian experience, for spiritual growth, and for entering more fully into the life and unity of the community.

Thus there are four continuous periods: the precatechumenate, the period for hearing the first preaching of the Gospel (nos. 36-40); the period of the catechumenate, set aside for a thorough catechesis and for the rites belonging to this period (nos. 75-104); the period of purification and enlightenment (Lenten preparation), designed for a more intense spiritual preparation, which is assisted by the celebration of the scrutinies and presentations (nos. 125-197); and the period of postbaptismal catechesis or mystagogy, marked by the new experience of sacraments and community (nos. 234-241).

8   The whole initiation must bear a markedly paschal character, since
the initiation of Christians is the first sacramental sharing in Christ's dying and ·rising and since, in addition, the period of purification and enlightenment ordinarily coincides with Lent[2] and the period of postbaptismal catechesis or mystagogy with the Easter season. All the resources of Lent should be brought to bear as a more intense preparation of the elect and the Easter Vigil should be regarded as the proper time for the sacraments of initiation. Because of pastoral needs, however, the sacraments of initiation may be celebrated at other times (see nos. 26-30).

MINISTRIES AND OFFICES

9   In light of what is said in *Christian Initiation*, General Introduction (no.
7), the people of God, as represented by the local Church, should understand and show by their concern that the initiation of adults is the responsibility of all the baptised.[3] Therefore the community must always be fully prepared in the pursuit of its apostolic vocation to give help to those who are searching for Christ. In the various circumstances of daily life, even as in the apostolate, all the followers of Christ have the obligation of spreading the faith according to their abilities.[4] Hence, the entire community must help the candidates and the catechumens throughout the process of initiation: during the period of the precatechumenate, the period of the catechumenate, the period of purification and enlightenment, and the period of postbaptismal catechesis or mystagogy. In particular:

1. During the period of evangelization and precatechumenate, the faithful should remember that for the Church and its members the

---

[2] See Vatican Council II, Constitution on the Liturgy *Sacrosanctum Concilium*, art. 109.

[3] See Vatican Council II, Decree on the Church's Missionary Activity *Ad gentes*, no. 14.

[4] See Vatican Council II, Dogmatic Constitution on the Church *Lumen gentium*, no. 17.

supreme purpose of the apostolate is that Christ's message is made known to the world by word and deed and that his grace is communicated.[5] They should therefore show themselves ready to give the candidates evidence of the spirit of the Christian community and to welcome them into their homes, into personal conversation, and into community gatherings.

2. At the celebrations belonging to the period of the catechumenate, the faithful should seek to be present whenever possible and should take an active part in the responses, prayers, singing, and acclamations.

3. On the day of election, because it is a day of growth for the community, the faithful, when called upon, should be sure to give honest and carefully considered testimony about the catechumens.

4. During Lent, the period of purification and enlightenment, the faithful should take care to participate in the rites of the scrutinies and presentations and give the elect the example of their own renewal in the spirit of penance, faith, and charity. At the Easter Vigil, they should attach great importance to renewing their own baptismal promises.

5. During the period immediately after baptism, the faithful should take part in the Masses for neophytes, that is, the Sunday Masses of the Easter season (see no. 25), welcome the neophytes with open arms in charity, and help them to feel more at home in the community of the baptised.

10   A sponsor accompanies any candidate seeking admission as a catechumen. Sponsors are persons who have known and assisted the candidates and stand as witnesses to the candidates' moral character, faith, and intention. It may happen that it is not the sponsor for the rite of acceptance and the period of the catechumenate but another person who serves as godparent for the periods of purification and enlightenment and of mystagogy.   42

11   Their godparents (for each a godmother or godfather, or both) accompany the candidates on the day of election, at the celebration of the sacraments of initiation, and during the period of mystagogy.[6] Godparents are persons chosen by the candidates on the basis of example, good qualities, and friendship, delegated by the local Christian community, and approved by the priest. It is the responsibility of godparents to show the candidates how to practise the Gospel in personal and social life, to sustain the candidates in moments of hesitancy and anxiety, to bear witness, and to guide the candidates' progress in the baptismal life. Chosen before the candidates' election, godparents fulfil this office publicly from the day of the rite of election, when they give testimony to the community about   43

---

[5] See Vatican Council II, Decree on the Apostolate of the Laity *Apostolicam actuositatem*, no. 6.
[6] See *Christian Initiation*, General Introduction, nos. 8 and 10, 1.

the candidates. They continue to be important during the time after reception of the sacraments when the neophytes need to be assisted so that they remain true to their baptismal promises.

12   The bishop,[7] in person or through his delegate, sets up, regulates, and promotes the programme of pastoral formation for catechumens and admits the candidates to their election and to the sacraments. It is hoped that, presiding if possible at the Lenten liturgy, he will himself celebrate the rite of election and, at the Easter Vigil, the sacraments of initiation, at least for the initiation of those who are fourteen years old or older. Finally, when pastoral care requires, the bishop should depute catechists, truly worthy and properly prepared, to celebrate the minor exorcisms (nos. 90-94) and the blessings of the catechumens (nos. 95-97). 44

13   Priests, in addition to their usual ministry for any celebration of baptism, confirmation, and the eucharist,[8] have the responsibility of attending to the pastoral and personal care of the catechumens,[9] especially those who seem hesitant and discouraged. With the help of deacons and catechists, they are to provide instruction for the catechumens; they are also to approve the choice of godparents and willingly listen to and help them; they are to be diligent in the correct celebration and adaptation of the rites throughout the entire course of Christian initiation (see no. 35). 45

14   The priest who baptises an adult or a child of catechetical age should, when the bishop is absent, also confer confirmation,[10] unless this sacrament is to be given at another time (see no. 24). When there are a large number of candidates to be confirmed, the minister of confirmation may associate priests with himself to administer the sacrament. It is preferable that the priests who are so invited: 46

1. either have a particular function or office in the diocese, being, namely, either vicars general, episcopal vicars, or district or regional vicars;

2. or be the parish priests (pastors) of the places where confirmation is conferred, parish priests (pastors) of the places where the candidates belong, or priests who have had a special part in the catechetical preparation of the candidates.[11]

15   Deacons should be ready to assist in the ministry to catechumens. Conferences of bishops that have decided in favour of the permanent diaconate should ensure that the number and distribution of permanent dea- 47

---

[7] See ibid., no. 12.

[8] See ibid., nos. 13-15.

[9] See Vatican Council II, Decree on the Ministry and Life of Priests *Presbyterorum Ordinis*, no. 6.

[10] See *Rite of Confirmation*, Introduction, no. 7, b.

[11] See ibid., no. 8.

cons are adequate for the carrying out of the steps, periods, and formation programs of the catechumenate wherever pastoral needs require.[12]

16   Catechists, who have an important office for the progress of the catechumens and for the growth of the community, should, whenever possible, have an active part in the rites. When deputed by the bishop (see no. 12), they may perform the minor exorcisms and blessings contained in the ritual.[13] When they are teaching, catechists should see that their instruction is filled with the spirit of the Gospel, adapted to the liturgical signs and the cycle of the Church's year, suited to the needs of the catechumens, and as far as possible enriched by local traditions.

TIME AND PLACE OF INITIATION

17   As a general rule, parish priests (pastors) should make use of the rite of initiation in such a way that the sacraments themselves are celebrated at the Easter Vigil and the rite of election takes place on the First Sunday of Lent. The rest of the rites are spaced on the basis of the structure and arrangement of the catechumenate as described previously (nos. 6-8). For pastoral needs of a more serious nature, however, it is lawful to arrange the schedule for the entire rite of initiation differently, as will be detailed later (nos. 26-30).

PROPER OR USUAL TIMES

18   The following should be noted about the time of celebrating the rite of acceptance into the order of catechumens (nos. 41-74).

  1. It should not be too early, but should be delayed until the candidates, according to their own dispositions and situation, have had sufficient time to conceive an initial faith and to show the first signs of conversion (see no. 42).

  2. In places where the number of candidates is smaller than usual, the rite of acceptance should be delayed until a group is formed that is sufficiently large for catechesis and the liturgical rites.

  3. Two dates in the year, or three if necessary, are to be fixed as the usual times for carrying out this rite.

19   The rite of election or enrolment of names (nos. 105-124) should as a rule be celebrated on the First Sunday of Lent. As circumstances suggest or require, it may be anticipated somewhat or even celebrated on a weekday.

---

[12] See Vatican Council II, Dogmatic Constitution on the Church *Lumen gentium*, no. 26; Decree on the Church's Missionary Activity *Ad gentes*, no. 16.

[13] See Vatican Council II, Constitution on the Liturgy *Sacrosanctum Concilium*, art. 79.

---

20   The scrutinies (nos. 137-143, 151-157, 158-164) should take place on the Third, Fourth, and Fifth Sundays of Lent, or, if necessary, on the other Sundays of Lent, or even on convenient weekdays. Three scrutinies should be celebrated. The bishop may dispense from one of them for serious reasons or, in extraordinary circumstances, even from two (see nos. 34,3, 307). When, for lack of time, the election is held early, the first scrutiny is also to be held early; but in this case care is to be taken not to prolong the period of purification and enlightenment beyond eight weeks. ⁵²

21   By ancient usage, the presentations, since they take place after the scrutinies, are part of the same period of purification and enlightenment. They are celebrated during the week. The presentation of the Creed to the catechumens (nos. 144-150) takes place during the week after the first scrutiny; the presentation of the Lord's Prayer (nos. 165-171) during the week after the third scrutiny. For pastoral reasons, however, to enrich the liturgy in the period of the catechumenate, each presentation may be transferred and celebrated during the period of the catechumenate as a kind of 'rite of passage' (see nos. 79, 103-104). ⁵³

22   On Holy Saturday, when the elect refrain from work and spend their time in recollection, the various preparation rites may be celebrated: the recitation or 'return' of the Creed by the elect, the ephphetha rite, the choosing of a Christian name, and even the anointing with the oil of catechumens (nos. 172-197). ⁵⁴

23   The celebration of the sacraments of Christian initiation (nos. 198-233) should take place at the Easter Vigil itself (see nos. 8, 17). But if there are a great many catechumens, the sacraments are given to the majority that night and reception of the sacraments by the rest may be transferred to days within the Easter octave, whether at the principal church or at a mission station. In this case either the Mass of the day or one of the ritual Masses 'Christian Initiation: Baptism' may be used and the readings are chosen from those of the Easter Vigil. ⁵⁵

24   In certain cases when there is serious reason, confirmation may be postponed until near the end of the period of postbaptismal catechesis, for example, Pentecost Sunday (see no. 239). ⁵⁶

25   On all the Sundays of the Easter season after Easter Sunday, the so-called Masses for neophytes are to be scheduled. The entire community and the newly baptised with their godparents should be encouraged to participate (see nos. 237-238). ⁵⁷

OUTSIDE THE USUAL TIMES

26   The entire rite of Christian initiation is normally arranged so that the sacraments will be celebrated during the Easter Vigil. Because of ⁵⁸

unusual circumstances and pastoral needs, however, the rite of election and the rites belonging to the period of purification and enlightenment may be held outside Lent and the sacraments of initiation may be celebrated at a time other than the Easter Vigil or Easter Sunday.

Even when the usual time has otherwise been observed, it is permissible, but only for serious pastoral needs (for example, if there are a great many people to be baptised), to choose a day other than the Easter Vigil or Easter Sunday, but preferably one during the Easter season, to celebrate the sacraments of initiation; the programme of initiation during Lent, however, must be maintained.

When the time is changed in either way, even though the rite of Christian initiation occurs at a different point in the liturgical year, the structure of the entire rite, with its properly spaced intervals, remains the same. But the following adjustments are made.

27   As far as possible, the sacraments of initiation are to be celebrated on a Sunday, using, as occasion suggests, the Sunday Mass or one of the ritual Masses 'Christian Initiation: Baptism' (see nos. 23, 200).

28   The rite of acceptance into the order of catechumens is to take place when the time is right (see no. 18).

29   The rite of election is to be celebrated about six weeks before the sacraments of initiation, so that there is sufficient time for the scrutinies and the presentations. Care should be taken not to schedule the celebration of the rite of election on a solemnity of the liturgical year.

30   The scrutinies should not be celebrated on solemnities, but on Sundays or even on weekdays, with the usual intervals.

Place of Celebration

31   The rites should be celebrated in the places appropriate to them as indicated in the ritual. Consideration should be given to special needs that arise in secondary stations of mission territories.

ADAPTATIONS BY THE CONFERENCES OF BISHOPS IN THE USE OF THE ROMAN RITUAL

32   In addition to the adaptations envisioned in *Christian Initiation*, General Introduction (nos. 30-33), the rite of Christian initiation of adults allows for other adaptations that will be decided by the conference of bishops.

33   Each conference of bishops has discretionary power to make the following decisions:

1. to establish for the precatechumenate, where it seems advisable, some way of receiving inquirers who are interested in the catechumenate (see no. 39);

2. to insert into the rite of acceptance into the order of catechumens a first exorcism and a renunciation of false worship, in regions where paganism is widespread (see nos. 69-72);

3. to decide that in the same rite the tracing of the sign of the cross upon the forehead (nos. 54-55) be replaced by making that sign in front of the forehead, in regions where the act of touching may not seem proper;

4. to decide that in the same rite candidates receive a new name in regions where it is the practise of non-Christian religions to give a new name to initiates immediately (no. 73);

5. to allow within the same rite, according to local customs, additional rites that symbolize reception into the community (no. 74);

6. to establish during the period of the catechumenate, in addition to the usual rites (nos. 81-97), 'rites of passage': for example, early celebration of the presentations (nos. 144-150, 165-171), the ephphetha rite (nos. 184-186), the catechumens' recitation of the Creed (nos. 180-183), or even an anointing of the catechumens (nos. 98-102);

7. to decide on the omission of the anointing with the oil of catechumens (no. 218) or its transferral to the preparation rites for Holy Saturday (nos. 190-194) or its use during the period of the catechumenate as a kind of 'rite of passage' (nos. 98-100);

8. to make more specific and detailed the formularies of renunciation for the rite of acceptance into the order of catechumens (nos. 70-72) and for the celebration of baptism (no. 217).

ADAPTATIONS BY THE BISHOP

34   It pertains to the bishop for his own diocese: 66

1. to set up the formation programme of the catechumenate and to lay down norms according to local needs (see no. 12);

2. to decide whether and when, as circumstances warrant, the entire rite of Christian initiation may be celebrated outside the usual times (see no. 26);

3. to dispense, on the basis of some serious obstacle, from one scrutiny or, in extraordinary circumstances, even from two (see no. 307);

4. to permit the simple rite to be used in whole or in part (see no. 307);

5. to depute catechists, truly worthy and properly prepared, to give the exorcisms and blessings (see nos. 12, 16);

6. to preside at the rite of election and to ratify, personally or through a delegate, the admission of the elect (see no. 12);

7. in keeping with the provisions of law,[14] to stipulate the requisite age for sponsors (see *Christian Initiation*, General Introduction, no. 10,2).

ADAPTATIONS BY THE MINISTER

35   Celebrants should make full and intelligent use of the freedom given to them either in *Christian Initiation*, General Introduction (no. 34) or in the rubrics of the rite itself. In many places the manner of acting or praying is intentionally left undetermined or two alternatives are offered, so that ministers, according to their prudent pastoral judgment, may accommodate the rite to the circumstances of the candidates and others who are present. In all the rites the greatest freedom is left in the invitations and instructions, and the intercessions may always be shortened, changed, or even expanded with new intentions, in order to fit the circumstances or special situation of the candidates (for example, a sad or joyful event occurring in a family) or of the others present (for example, sorrow or joy common to the parish or civic community).

The minister will also adapt the texts by changing the gender and number as required.

---

[14] See *Codex Iuris Canonici*, can. 874, §1, 2°.

PART I
CHRISTIAN INITIATION
OF ADULTS

*Our Saviour Jesus Christ has done away with death
and brought us life through his Gospel*

OUTLINE FOR CHRISTIAN INITIATION OF ADULTS

PERIOD OF EVANGELIZATION AND PRECATECHUMENATE

This is a time, of no fixed duration or structure, for inquiry and introduction to gospel values, an opportunity for the beginnings of faith.

FIRST STEP: ACCEPTANCE INTO THE ORDER OF CATECHUMENS

This is the liturgical rite, usually celebrated on some annual date or dates, marking the beginning of the catechumenate proper, as the candidates express and the Church accepts their intention to respond to God's call to follow the way of Christ.

PERIOD OF THE CATECHUMENATE

This is the time, in duration corresponding to the progress of the individual, for the nurturing and growth of the catechumens' faith and conversion to God; celebrations of the word and prayers of exorcism and blessing are meant to assist the process.

SECOND STEP: ELECTION OR ENROLMENT OF NAMES

This is the liturgical rite, usually celebrated on the First Sunday of Lent, by which the Church formally ratifies the catechumens' readiness for the sacraments of initiation and the catechumens, now the elect, express the will to receive these sacraments.

PERIOD OF PURIFICATION AND ENLIGHTENMENT

This is the time immediately preceding the elects' initiation, usually the Lenten season preceding the celebration of this initiation at the Easter Vigil; it is a time of reflection, intensely centred on conversion, marked by celebration of the scrutinies and presentations and of the preparation rites on Holy Saturday.

THIRD STEP: CELEBRATION OF THE SACRAMENTS OF INITIATION

This is the liturgical rite, usually integrated into the Easter Vigil, by which the elect are initiated through baptism, confirmation, and the eucharist.

PERIOD OF POSTBAPTISMAL CATECHESIS OR MYSTAGOGY

This is the time, usually the Easter season, following the celebration of initiation, during which the newly initiated experience being fully a part of the Christian community by means of both pertinent catechesis and particularly by participation with all the faithful in the Sunday eucharistic celebration.

PERIOD OF EVANGELIZATION AND PRECATECHUMENATE

*I, the light, have come into the world, so that whoever believes in me
need not remain in the dark any more*

36   Although the rite of initiation begins with admission to the catechu-   9
menate, the preceding period or precatechumenate is of great importance
and as a rule should not be omitted. It is a time of evangelization: faithfully and constantly the living God is proclaimed and Jesus Christ whom
he has sent for the salvation of all. Thus those who are not yet Christians,
their hearts opened by the Holy Spirit, may believe and be freely converted
to the Lord and commit themselves sincerely to him. For he who is the
way, the truth, and the life fulfils all their spiritual expectations, indeed
infinitely surpasses them.[1]

37   From evangelization, completed with the help of God, come the faith   10
and initial conversion that cause a person to feel called away from sin and
drawn into the mystery of God's love. The whole period of the precatechumenate is set aside for this evangelization, so that the genuine will
to follow Christ and seek baptism may mature.

38   During this period, priests and deacons, catechists and other lay-   11
persons are to give the candidates a suitable explanation of the Gospel (see
no. 42). The candidates are to receive help and attention so that with a
purified and clearer intention they may cooperate with God's grace. Op-
portunities should be provided for them to meet families and other groups
of Christians.

39   It belongs to the conference of bishops to provide for the evangeliza-   12
tion proper to this period. The conference may also provide, if circumstances suggest and in keeping with local custom, a preliminary manner
of receiving those interested in the precatechumenate, that is, those inquirers
who, even though they do not fully believe, show some leaning toward the
Christian faith (and who may be called 'sympathisers').

  1. Such a reception, if it takes place, will be carried out without any
  ritual celebration; it is the expression not yet of faith, but of a right
  intention.

  2. The reception will be adapted to local conditions and to the pastoral situation. Some candidates may need to see evidence of the spirit
  of Christians that they are striving to understand and experience. For
  others, however, whose catechumenate will be delayed for one reason

---

[1] See Vatican Council II, Decree on the Church's Missionary Activity *Ad gentes*, no. 13.

or another, some initial act of the candidates or the community that expresses their reception may be appropriate.

3. The reception will be held at a meeting or gathering of the local community, on an occasion that will permit friendly conversation. An inquirer or 'sympathiser' is introduced by a friend and then welcomed and received by the priest or some other representative member of the community.

40   During the precatechumenate period, parish priests (pastors) should help those taking part in it with prayers suited to them, for example, by celebrating for their spiritual well-being the prayers of exorcism and the blessings given in the ritual (nos. 94, 97).

FIRST STEP: ACCEPTANCE INTO THE ORDER OF CATECHUMENS

Lord, let your mercy be on us, as we place our trust in you

41   The rite that is called the rite of acceptance into the order of catechumens is of the utmost importance. Assembling publicly for the first time, the candidates who have completed the period of the precatechumenate declare their intention to the Church and the Church in turn, carrying out its apostolic mission, accepts them as persons who intend to become its members. God showers his grace on the candidates, since the celebration manifests their desire publicly and marks their reception and first consecration by the Church.

14
15
68

42   The prerequisite for making this first step is that the beginnings of the spiritual life and the fundamentals of Christian teaching have taken root in the candidates.[1] Thus there must be evidence of the first faith that was conceived during the period of evangelization and precatechumenate and of an initial conversion and intention to change their lives and to enter into a relationship with God in Christ. Consequently, there must also be evidence of the first stirrings of repentance, a start to the practice of calling upon God in prayer, a sense of the Church, and some experience of the company and spirit of Christians through contact with a priest or with members of the community. The candidate should also be instructed about the celebration of the liturgical rite of acceptance.

15
68

43   Before the rite is celebrated, therefore, sufficient and necessary time, as required in each case, should be set aside to evaluate and, if necessary, to purify the candidates' motives and dispositions. With the help of the sponsors (see no. 10), catechists, and deacons, parish priests (pastors) have the responsibility for judging the outward indications of such dispositions.[2] Because of the effect of baptism once validly received (see *Christian Initiation*, General Introduction, no. 4), it is the duty of parish priests (pastors) to see to it that no baptised person seeks for any reason whatever to be baptised a second time.

16
69

44   The rite will take place on specified days during the year (see no. 18) that are suited to local conditions. The rite consists in the reception of the candidates, the celebration of the word of God, and the dismissal of the candidates; celebration of the eucharist may follow.

By decision of the conference of bishops, the following may be incorporated into this rite: a first exorcism and renunciation of false worship

65
69
72

---

[1] See Vatican Council II, Decree on the Church's Missionary Activity *Ad gentes*, no. 14.

[2] See ibid., no. 13.

(nos. 70-72), the giving of a new name (no. 73), and additional rites signifying reception into the community (no. 74).

45   It is desirable that the entire Christian community or some part of it, consisting of friends and acquaintances, catechists and priests, take an active part in the celebration. The presiding celebrant is a priest or a deacon. The sponsors should also attend in order to present to the Church the candidates they have brought.

46   After the celebration of the rite of acceptance, the names of the catechumens are to be duly inscribed in the register of catechumens, along with the names of the sponsors and the minister and the date and place of the celebration.

47   From this time on the Church embraces the catechumens as its own with a mother's love and concern. Joined to the Church, the catechumens are now part of the household of Christ,[3] since the Church nourishes them with the word of God and sustains them by means of liturgical celebrations. The catechumens should be eager, then, to take part in celebrations of the word of God and to receive blessings and other sacramentals. When two catechumens marry or when a catechumen marries an unbaptised person, the appropriate rite is to be used.[4] One who dies during the catechumenate receives a Christian burial.

---

[3] See Vatican Council II, Dogmatic Constitution on the Church *Lumen gentium*, no. 14; Decree on the Church's Missionary Activity *Ad gentes*, no. 14.

[4] See *Rite of Marriage*, nos. 55-66.

OUTLINE OF THE RITE

RECEIVING THE CANDIDATES

Greeting
Opening Dialogue
Candidates' First Acceptance of the Gospel
Affirmation by the Sponsors and the Assembly
Signing of the Candidates with the Cross
  Signing of the Forehead
  [Signing of the Other Senses]
  Concluding Prayer
Invitation to the Celebration of the Word of God

LITURGY OF THE WORD

Instruction
Readings
Homily
[Presentation of a Bible]
Intercessions for the Catechumens
Prayer over the Catechumens
Dismissal of the Catechumens

LITURGY OF THE EUCHARIST

RITE OF ACCEPTANCE INTO THE ORDER OF CATECHUMENS

RECEIVING THE CANDIDATES

48   The candidates, their sponsors, and a group of the faithful   73
gather outside the church (or inside at the entrance or elsewhere)
or at some other site suitable for this rite. As the priest or deacon, wearing an alb or surplice, a stole, and, if desired, a cope
of festive colour, goes to meet them, the assembly of the faithful
may sing a psalm or an appropriate song.

GREETING

49   The celebrant greets the candidates in a friendly manner.   74
He speaks to them, their sponsors, and all present, pointing out
the joy and happiness of the Church. He may also recall for the
sponsors and friends the particular experience and religious response by which the candidates, following their own spiritual path,
have come to this first step.

Then he invites the sponsors and candidates to come forward.
As they are taking their places before the celebrant, an appropriate song may be sung, for example, Psalm 62(63):1-8.

OPENING DIALOGUE

50   Unless the candidates are already known to all present, the   75
celebrant asks for or calls out their given names. The candidates
answer one by one, even if, because of a large number, the question is asked only once. One of the following or something similar may be used.

A   The celebrant asks:

What is your name?

Candidate:

N.

B   The celebrant calls out the name of each candidate.

The candidate answers:

Present.

The celebrant continues with the following questions for the individual candidates or, when there are a large number, for the candidates to answer as a group. The celebrant may use other words than those provided in asking the candidates about their intentions and may let them answer in their own words: for example, to the first question, 'What do you ask of the Church of God?' or 'What do you desire?' or 'For what reason have you come?', he may receive such answers as 'The grace of Christ' or 'Entrance into the Church' or 'Eternal life' or other suitable responses. The celebrant then phrases his next question according to the answer received.

Celebrant:

What do you ask of God's Church?

Candidate:

Faith.

Celebrant:

What does faith offer you?

Candidate:

Eternal life.

> 51   By decision of the conference of bishops, the candidates' first acceptance of the Gospel (no. 52) may be replaced by the rite of exorcism and renunciation of false worship (nos. 70-72).

CANDIDATES' FIRST ACCEPTANCE OF THE GOSPEL

52   The celebrant addresses the candidates, adapting one of the following formularies or similar words to the answers received in the opening dialogue.   76

A   **God gives light to everyone who comes into this world; though**   76
unseen, he reveals himself through the works of his hand, so
that all people may learn to give thanks to their Creator.

You have followed God's light and the way of the Gospel now
lies open before you. Set your feet firmly on that path and ac-

---

knowledge the living God, who truly speaks to everyone. Walk in the light of Christ and learn to trust in his wisdom. Commit your lives daily to his care, so that you may come to believe in him with all your heart.

This is the way of faith along which Christ will lead you in love toward eternal life. Are you prepared to begin this journey today under the guidance of Christ?

Candidates:

I am.

B   God is our Creator and in him all living things have their exis-   370:1
tence. He enlightens our minds, so that we may come to know and worship him. He has sent his faithful witness, Jesus Christ, to announce to us what he has seen and heard, the mysteries of heaven and earth.

Since you acknowledge with joy that Christ has come, now is the time to hear his word, so that you may possess eternal life by beginning, in our company, to know God and to love your neigbour. Are you ready, with the help of God, to live this life?

Candidates:

I am.

C   This is eternal life: to know the one true God and Jesus Christ,   370:2
whom he has sent. Christ has been raised from the dead and appointed by God as the Lord of life and ruler of all things, seen and unseen.

If, then, you wish to become his disciples and members of his Church, you must be guided to the fulness of the truth that he has revealed to us. You must learn to make the mind of Christ Jesus your own. You must strive to pattern your life on the teachings of the Gospel and so to love the Lord your God and your neigbour. For this was Christ's command and he was its perfect example.

Is each of you ready to accept these teachings of the Gospel?

Candidates:

I am.

Affirmation by the Sponsors and the Assembly

> 53 Then the celebrant turns to the sponsors and the assembly
> and asks them in these or similar words.

77
81

Sponsors, you now present these candidates to us; are you, and all who are gathered here with us, ready to help these candidates find and follow Christ?

> All:

We are.

> With hands joined, the celebrant says:

Father of mercy,
we thank you for these your servants.
You have sought and summoned them in many ways
and they have turned to seek you.

82

You have called them today
and they have answered in our presence:
we praise you, Lord, and we bless you.

> All sing or say:

We praise you, Lord, and we bless you.

Signing of the Candidates with the Cross

> 54 Next the cross is traced on the forehead of the candidates
> (or in front of the forehead, if the conference of bishops deems
> this more suitable); at the discretion of the celebrant the sign-
> ing of one, several, or all of the senses may follow. The celebrant
> alone says the formularies accompanying each signing.

83
85

Signing of the Forehead

> 55 One of the following options is used, depending on the num-
> ber of candidates.

A   If there are only a few candidates, the celebrant invites them and   83
their sponsors in these or similar words.

**Come forward now with your sponsors to receive the sign of
your new way of life as catechumens.**

With their sponsors, the candidates come one by one to the celebrant; with his thumb he traces a cross on the forehead; then,
if there is to be no signing of the senses, the sponsor does the
same. The celebrant says:

**N., receive the cross on your forehead.
It is Christ himself who now strengthens you
with this sign of his love.
Learn to know him and follow him.**

All sing or say the following or another suitable acclamation.   86

Glory and praise to you, Lord Jesus Christ!

B   If there are a great many candidates, the celebrant speaks to them   84
in these or similar words.*

**Dear candidates, your answers mean that you wish to share our
life and hope in Christ. To admit you as catechumens I now
mark you with the sign of Christ's cross and call upon your
catechists and sponsors to do the same. The whole community
welcomes you with love and stands ready to help you.**

Then the celebrant makes the sign of the cross over all together,
as a cross is traced by a sponsor or catechist on the forehead of
each candidate. The celebrant says:

**Receive the cross on your forehead.
It is Christ himself who now strengthens you
with this sign of his love.**
Learn to know him and follow him.**

All sing or say the following or another suitable acclamation.   86

Glory and praise to you, Lord Jesus Christ!

---

* In regions where a renunciation of false worship (no. 72) has been included in the rite of acceptance: 'Dear
candidates, your answers mean that you have rejected false worship and wish to share our life and hope in
Christ. . . .'

** In regions where there has been a renunciation of false worship: 'with this sign of his victory.'

Signing of the Other Senses

56 The signing is carried out by the catechists or the sponsors.
(If required by special circumstances, this may be done by assisting priests or deacons.) The signing of each sense may be
followed by an acclamation in praise of Christ, for example, 'Glory
and praise to you, Lord Jesus Christ!'

While the ears are being signed, the celebrant says:

**Receive the sign of the cross on your ears,
that you may hear the voice of the Lord.**

While the eyes are being signed:

**Receive the sign of the cross on your eyes,
that you may see the glory of God.**

While the lips are being signed:

**Receive the sign of the cross on your lips,
that you may respond to the word of God.**

While the breast is being signed:

**Receive the sign of the cross over your heart,
that Christ may dwell there by faith.**

While the shoulders are being signed:

**Receive the sign of the cross on your shoulders,
that you may bear the gentle yoke of Christ.**

Without touching them, the celebrant alone makes the sign of
the cross over all the candidates at once (or, if they are few, over
each individually), saying:

**I sign you with the sign of eternal life
in the name of the Father, and of the Son, ✠
and of the Holy Spirit.**

Catechumens:

Amen.

Concluding Prayer

57 The celebrant concludes the signing of the forehead (and
senses) with one of the following prayers.

Let us pray.

A   Lord, 87
we have signed these catechumens
with the sign of Christ's cross.

Protect them by its power,
so that, faithful to the grace which has begun in them,
they may keep your commandments
and come to the glory of rebirth in baptism.

We ask this through Christ our Lord.

R. Amen.

B   Almighty God, 87
by the cross and resurrection of your Son
you have given life to your people.

Your servants have received the sign of the cross:
make them living proof of its saving power
and help them to persevere in the footsteps of Christ.

We ask this through Christ our Lord.

R. Amen.

> 58   At this point, by decision of the conference of bishops, the giving of a new name (no. 73) may take place.
>
> 59   By decision of the conference of bishops, the invitation to the celebration of the word of God may be preceded or followed by the additional rites signifying reception into the community (no. 74).

INVITATION TO THE CELEBRATION OF THE WORD OF GOD

60   The celebrant next invites the catechumens and their sponsors to enter the church (or the place where the liturgy of the word will be celebrated). He uses the following or similar words, accompanying them with some gesture of invitation. 90

N. and N., come into the church,
to share with us at the table of God's word.

During the entry an appropriate song is sung or the following antiphon with Psalm 33(34):2, 3, 6, 9, 10, 11, 16.

Come, my children, and listen to me;
I will teach you the fear of the Lord.

LITURGY OF THE WORD

INSTRUCTION

91

61 After the catechumens have reached their places, the celebrant speaks to them briefly, helping them to understand the dignity of God's word, which is proclaimed and heard in the church.

The Lectionary for Mass or the Bible is carried in procession and placed with honour on the lectern, where it may be incensed.

Celebration of the liturgy of the word follows.

READINGS

92
37?

62 The readings may be chosen from any of the readings in the Lectionary for Mass that are suited to the new catechumens or the following (Lectionary, Vol. III, pp. 3-5) may be used.

FIRST READING
Genesis 12:1-4a — *Leave your country for the land I will show you.*

RESPONSORIAL PSALM
Psalm 33:4-5, 12-13, 18-19, 20 and 22
R. (v.12b) **Happy the people the Lord has chosen as his own.**
Or:
R. (v.22) **May your love be upon us, O Lord,**
as we place all our hope in you.

VERSE BEFORE THE GOSPEL
John 1:41, 17b
We have found the Messiah — which means the Christ —
grace and truth have come through him.

GOSPEL
John 1:35-42 — *Look, there is the lamb of God. We have found the Messiah.*

HOMILY

92

63 A homily follows that explains the readings.

PRESENTATION OF A BIBLE

93

64 A book containing the Gospels may be given to the catechumens by the celebrant; a cross may also be given, unless this has already been done as one of the additional rites (see no. 74). The celebrant may use words suited to the gift presented, for example, 'Receive the Gospel of Jesus Christ, the Son of God,' and the catechumens may respond in an appropriate way.

INTERCESSIONS FOR THE CATECHUMENS

65   Then the sponsors and the whole congregation join in the following or a similar formulary of intercession for the catechumens.

[If it is decided, in accord with no. 68, that after the dismissal of the catechumens the usual general intercessions of the Mass are to be omitted and that the liturgy of the eucharist is to begin immediately, intentions for the Church and the whole world are to be added to the following intentions for the catechumens.]

Celebrant:

These catechumens, who are our brothers and sisters, have already travelled a long road. We rejoice with them in the gentle guidance of God who has brought them to this day. Let us pray that they may press onwards, until they come to share fully in our way of life.

Assisting minister:

That God our Father may reveal his Christ to them more and more with every passing day, let us pray to the Lord:

R. Lord, hear our prayer.

Assisting minister:

That they may undertake with generous hearts and souls whatever God may ask of them, let us pray to the Lord:

R. Lord, hear our prayer.

Assisting minister:

That they may have our sincere and unfailing support every step of the way, let us pray to the Lord:

R. Lord, hear our prayer.

Assisting minister:

That they may find in our community compelling signs of unity and generous love, let us pray to the Lord:

R. Lord, hear our prayer.

Assisting minister:

That their hearts and ours may become more responsive to the needs of others, let us pray to the Lord:

R. Lord, hear our prayer.

Assisting minister:

That in due time they may be found worthy to receive the baptism of new birth and renewal in the Holy Spirit, let us pray to the Lord:

R. Lord, hear our prayer.

PRAYER OVER THE CATECHUMENS

66 After the intercessions, the celebrant, with hands outstretched over the catechumens, says one of the following prayers.

95

Let us pray.

A   [God of our forebears and] God of all creation,   95
we ask you to look favourably on your servants N. and N.;
make them fervent in spirit,
joyful in hope,
and always ready to serve your name.

Lead them, Lord, to the baptism of new birth,
so that, living a fruitful life in the company of your faithful,
they may receive the eternal reward that you promise.

We ask this in the name of Jesus the Lord.

R. Amen.

B   Almighty God,   95
source of all creation,
you have made us in your image.
Welcome with love those who come before you today.

They have listened among us to the word of Christ;
by its power renew them
and by your grace refashion them,
so that in time they may assume the full likeness of Christ,
who lives and reigns for ever and ever.

R. Amen.

DISMISSAL OF THE CATECHUMENS

67 If the eucharist is to be celebrated, the catechumens are normally dismissed at this point by use of option A; if the catechumens are to stay for the celebration of the eucharist, option B

96

is used; if the eucharist is not to be celebrated, the entire assembly is dismissed by use of option C.

A   The celebrant recalls briefly the great joy with which the catechumens have just been received and urges them to live according to the word of God they have just heard. After the dismissal formulary, the group of catechumens goes out but does not disperse. With the help of some of the faithful, the catechumens remain together to share their joy and spiritual experiences. For the dismissal the following or similar words are used.

**Catechumens, go in peace,
and may the Lord remain with you always.**

Catechumens:
Thanks be to God.

B   If for serious reasons the catechumens cannot leave (see no. 75,3) and must remain with the baptised, they are to be instructed that though they are present at the eucharist, they cannot take part in it as the baptised do. They may be reminded of this by the celebrant in these or similar words.   96

Although you cannot yet participate fully in the Lord's eucharist, stay with us as a sign of our hope that all God's children will eat and drink with the Lord and work with the Holy Spirit to re-create the face of the earth.

C   The celebrant dismisses those present, using these or similar words.

**Go in peace,
and may the Lord remain with you always.**

All:
Thanks be to God.

An appropriate song may conclude the celebration.

LITURGY OF THE EUCHARIST

When the eucharist is to follow, intercessory prayer is resumed with the usual general intercessions for the needs of the Church and the whole world; then, if required, the profession of faith is said. But for pastoral reasons these general intercessions and the profession of faith may be omitted. The liturgy of the eucharist then begins as usual with the preparation of the gifts.   97

OPTIONAL RITES FOR PARTICULAR REGIONS

69 By decision of the conference of bishops any or all of the following may be incorporated into the 'Rite of Acceptance into the Order of Catechumens.'

Exorcism and Renunciation of False Worship

7&

70 In regions where false worship is widespread, whether in worshipping spiritual powers or in calling on the shades of the dead or in using magical arts, the conference of bishops may introduce a first exorcism and a renunciation of false worship; this replaces the candidates' first acceptance of the Gospel (no. 52).

Exorcism

7'

71 After giving a brief introduction to the rite, the celebrant breathes lightly toward the face of each candidate and, with a symbolic gesture, for example, holding up his right hand, or without any gesture, says the formulary of exorcism.

[If there are a great many candidates, the breathing is omitted and the formulary said only once; the breathing is also omitted in places where it would be unacceptable.]

Celebrant:

**By the breath of your mouth, O Lord,
drive away the spirits of evil.
Command them to depart,
for your kingdom has come among us.**

Renunciation of False Worship

8C

72 If the conference of bishops judges it suitable to have the candidate openly renounce false worship and spirits or magical arts, the conference should prepare a formulary for the questions and renunciation relevant to the local situation. As long as the language is not offensive to members of other religious groups, this may be expressed using one of the following formularies or similar words.

A   Celebrant: 80

Dear candidates, you have set out toward your baptism. You have answered God's call and been helped by his grace; you have decided to serve and worship him alone and the one he has sent, Jesus Christ. Since you have made this choice, now is the time to renounce publicly those powers that are not of God and those forms of worship that do not rightly honour him. Are you, therefore, resolved to remain loyal to God and his Christ and never to serve ungodly powers?

Candidates:
Yes, we are.

Celebrant:
Do you reject the worship of N. and N.?

Candidates:
Yes, we do.

He continues in the same way for each form of worship to be renounced.

B   Celebrant: 371

Dear candidates, the true God has called you and led you here. You sincerely desire to worship and serve him alone, and his Son Jesus Christ. Now, in the presence of this community, you must reject all rites and forms of worship that do not honour the true God. Are you determined never to abandon him and his Son, Jesus Christ, and never to return to the service of other masters?

Candidates:
We are.

Celebrant:
Christ Jesus, Lord of the living and the dead, has power over all spirits and demons. Are you determined never to abandon him and never again to serve N.*?

Candidates:
We are.

---

* Here mention is made of the images worshipped in false rites, such as fetishes.

Celebrant:

Christ Jesus alone has the power to protect us. Are you determined never to abandon him and never again to seek [wear/use] N.*?

Candidates:

We are.

Celebrant:

Christ Jesus alone is truth. Are you determined never to abandon him and never to seek out soothsayers, magicians, or witch doctors?

Candidates:

We are.

The celebration then continues with the affirmation by the sponsors and the assembly (no. 53).

Giving of a New Name

73   In regions where local non-Christian religions have the practise of giving a new name to new members, the conference of bishops may decide that after the signing of the candidates with the cross (nos. 54-56), the catechumens may be given a new name.** This may be either a Christian name or one familiar in the culture, provided such a name is not incompatible with Christian beliefs. (In some cases it will suffice to explain the Christian understanding of the catechumens' given names.) If a new name is given, one of the following formularies may be used.

A   Celebrant:

By what name do you wish to be called?

Catechumen:

N.

---

* Here mention is made of the objects that are used superstitiously, such as amulets.

** If so, this rite is not repeated on Holy Saturday; see no. 187.

B   Celebrant:

N., from now on you will [also] be called N.

The catechumen gives the following or another suitable reply.

Amen.

The celebration then continues with the additional rites (no. 74)
or the invitation to the celebration of the word of God (no. 60).

ADDITIONAL RITES

74   Practises that seem suitable as signs of the catechumens'   89
reception into the community, such as the giving of salt or some
other symbolic act, or even the presentation of a cross or a religious medal, may be introduced at the discretion of the conference of bishops and incorporated into the rite either before or
after the invitation to the celebration of the word of God (no. 60).

PERIOD OF THE CATECHUMENATE

Leave your country, and come into the land I will show you

75 The catechumenate is an extended period during which the candidates are given suitable pastoral formation and guidance, aimed at training them in the Christian life.[1] In this way, the dispositions manifested at their acceptance into the catechumenate are brought to maturity. This is achieved in four ways.

1. A suitable catechesis is provided by priests or deacons, or by catechists and others of the faithful, planned to be gradual and complete in its coverage, accommodated to the liturgical year, and solidly supported by celebrations of the word. This catechesis leads the catechumens not only to an appropriate acquaintance with dogmas and precepts but also to a profound sense of the mystery of salvation in which they desire to participate.

2. As they become familiar with the Christian way of life and are helped by the example and support of sponsors, godparents, and the entire Christian community, the catechumens learn to turn more readily to God in prayer, to bear witness to the faith, in all things to keep their hopes set on Christ, to follow supernatural inspiration in their deeds, and to practise love of neighbour, even at the cost of self-renunciation. Thus formed, 'the newly converted set out on a spiritual journey. Already sharing through faith in the mystery of Christ's death and resurrection, they pass from the old to a new nature made perfect in Christ. Since this transition brings with it a progressive change of outlook and conduct, it should become manifest by means of its social consequences and it should develop gradually during the period of the catechumenate. Since the Lord in whom they believe is a sign of contradiction, the newly converted often experience divisions and separations, but they also taste the joy that God gives without measure.'[2]

3. The Church, like a mother, helps the catechumens on their journey by means of suitable liturgical rites, which purify the catechumens little by little and strengthen them with God's blessing. Celebrations of the word of God are arranged for their benefit, and at Mass they may also take part with the faithful in the liturgy of the word, thus better preparing themselves for their eventual participation in the liturgy of the eucharist. Ordinarily, however, when they are present in the assembly of the faithful they should be kindly dis-

---

[1] See Vatican Council II, Decree on the Church's Missionary Activity *Ad gentes*, no. 14.

[2] Ibid., no. 13.

missed before the liturgy of the eucharist begins (unless their dismissal would present practical or pastoral problems). For they must await their baptism, which will join them to God's priestly people and empower them to participate in Christ's new worship.

4. Since the Church's life is apostolic, catechumens should also learn how to work actively with others to spread the Gospel and build up the Church by the witness of their lives and by professing their faith.[3]

76 The duration of the catechumenate will depend on the grace of God and on various circumstances, such as the programme of instruction for the catechumenate, the number of catechists, deacons, and priests, the cooperation of the individual catechumens, the means necessary for them to come to the site of the catechumenate and spend time there, the help of the local community. Nothing, therefore, can be settled a priori.

The time spent in the catechumenate should be long enough — several years if necessary — for the conversion and faith of the catechumens to become strong. By their formation in the entire Christian life and a sufficiently prolonged probation the catechumens are properly initiated into the mysteries of salvation and the practise of an evangelical way of life. By means of sacred rites celebrated at successive times they are led into the life of faith, worship, and charity belonging to the people of God.

77 It is the responsibility of the bishop to fix the duration and to direct the programme of the catechumenate. The conference of bishops, after considering the conditions of its people and region,[4] may also wish to provide specific guidelines. At the discretion of the bishop, on the basis of the spiritual preparation of the candidate, the period of the catechumenate may in particular cases be shortened (see nos. 307, 308-311); in altogether extraordinary cases the catechumenate may be completed all at once (see nos. 308, 312-345).

78 The instruction that the catechumens receive during this period should be of a kind that while presenting Catholic teaching in its entirety also enlightens faith, directs the heart toward God, fosters participation in the liturgy, inspires apostolic activity, and nurtures a life completely in accord with the spirit of Christ.

79 Among the rites belonging to the period of the catechumenate, then, celebrations of the word of God (nos. 81-89) are foremost. The minor exorcisms (nos. 90-94) and the blessings of the catechumens (nos. 95-97) are ordinarily celebrated in conjunction with a celebration of the word. In addition, other rites may be celebrated to mark the passage of the catechumens from one level of catechesis to another: for example, an anointing

---

[3] See Vatican Council II, Decree on the Church's Missionary Activity *Ad gentes*, no. 14.
[4] See Vatican Council II, Constitution on the Liturgy *Sacrosanctum Concilium*, art. 64.

---

of the catechumens may be celebrated (nos. 98-102) and the presentations of the Creed and the Lord's Prayer may be anticipated (see nos. 103-104).

80   During the period of the catechumenate, the catechumens should give thought to choosing the godparents who will present them to the Church on the day of their election (see no. 11; also *Christian Initiation*, General Introduction, nos. 8-10). 104 105

Provision should also be made for the entire community involved in the formation of the catechumens — priests, deacons, catechists, sponsors, godparents, friends and neighbours — to participate in some of the celebrations belonging to the catechumenate, including any of the optional 'rites of passage' (nos. 98-104).

RITES BELONGING TO THE PERIOD OF THE CATECHUMENATE

CELEBRATIONS OF THE WORD OF GOD

81   During the period of the catechumenate there should be celebrations of the word of God that accord with the liturgical season and that contribute to the instruction of the catechumens and the needs of the community. These celebrations of the word are: first, celebrations held specially for the catechumens; second, participation in the liturgy of the word at the Sunday Mass; third, celebrations held in connection with catechetical instruction.

82   The special celebrations of the word of God arranged for the benefit of the catechumens have as their main purpose:

> 1. to implant in their hearts the teachings they are receiving: for example, the morality characteristic of the New Testament, the forgiving of injuries and insults, a sense of sin and repentance, the duties Christians must carry out in the world;
>
> 2. to give them instruction and experience in the different aspects and ways of prayer;
>
> 3. to explain to them the signs, celebrations, and seasons of the liturgy;
>
> 4. to prepare them gradually to enter the worship assembly of the entire community.

83   From the very beginning of the period of the catechumenate the catechumens should be taught to keep holy the Lord's Day.

> 1. Care should be taken that some of the special celebrations of the word just mentioned (no. 82) are held on Sunday, so that the catechumens will become accustomed to taking an active and practised part in these celebrations.
>
> 2. Gradually the catechumens should be admitted to the first part of the celebration of the Sunday Mass. After the liturgy of the word they should, if possible, be dismissed, but an intention for them is included in the general intercessions.

84   Celebrations of the word may also be held in connection with catechetical or instructional meetings of the catechumens, so that these will occur in a context of prayer.

Model for a Celebration of the Word of God

85   For the celebrations of the word of God that are held specially for the benefit of the catechumens (see no. 82), the following structure (nos. 86-89) may be used as a model.

86   Song: An appropriate song may be sung to open the celebration.

87   Readings: One or more readings from Scripture, chosen for their relevance to the formation of the catechumens, are proclaimed by a baptised member of the community.

88   Homily: A brief homily that explains and applies the readings should be given.

89   Concluding Rites: The celebration of the word may conclude with a minor exorcism (no. 94) after the homily or with a blessing of the catechumens (no. 97) or with both; if a rite of anointing (nos. 101-102) is adopted as an option, it may replace the minor exorcism and may also be followed by one of the blessings (no. 97).*

---

* Celebrations of the word that are held in connection with instructional sessions may include, along with an appropriate reading, a minor exorcism (no. 94) or a blessing of the catechumens (no. 97) or both.

   The meetings of the catechumens after the liturgy of the word of the Sunday Mass may also include a minor exorcism (no. 94) or a blessing (no. 97) or both.

MINOR EXORCISMS

90   The first or minor exorcisms have been composed in the form of petitions directly addressed to God. They draw the attention of the catechumens to the real nature of Christian life, the struggle between flesh and spirit, the importance of self-denial for reaching the blessedness of God's kingdom, and the unending need for God's help.

91   The presiding celebrant for the minor exorcisms is a priest, a deacon, or a qualified catechist appointed by the bishop for this ministry (see no. 16).

92   The minor exorcisms take place within a celebration of the word of God held in a church, a chapel, or in a centre for the catechumenate. A minor exorcism may also be held at the beginning or end of a meeting for catechesis. When there is some special need, one of these prayers of exorcism may be said privately for individual catechumens.

93   The formularies for the minor exorcisms may be used on several occasions, as different situations may suggest.

PRAYERS OF EXORCISM

> 94   As the catechumens bow or kneel, the celebrant, with hands outstretched over them, says one of the following prayers.

Let us pray.

A   God of power,
      who promised us the Holy Spirit through Jesus your Son,
      we pray to you for these catechumens,
      who present themselves before you.

      Protect them from the spirit of evil
      and guard them against error and sin,
      so that they may become the temple of your Holy Spirit.

      Confirm what we profess in faith,
      so that our words may not be empty,
      but full of the grace and power
      by which your Son has freed the world.

      We ask this through Christ our Lord.

      R. Amen.

B   Lord our God,
      you make known the true life;

you cut away corruption and strengthen faith,
you build up hope and foster love.

In the name of your beloved Son,
our Lord Jesus Christ,
and in the power of the Holy Spirit,
we ask you to remove from these your servants
all unbelief and hesitation in faith,
[the worship of false gods and magic,
witchcraft and dealings with the dead],
the love of money and lawless passions,
enmity and quarrelling,
and every manner of evil.

And because you have called them
to be holy and sinless in your sight,
create in them a spirit of faith and reverence,
of patience and hope,
of temperance and purity,
and of charity and peace.

We ask this through Christ our Lord.

R. Amen.

C   God of power, 115
you created us in your image and likeness
and formed us in holiness and justice.

Even when we sinned against you,
you did not abandon us,
but in your wisdom chose to save us
by the incarnation of your Son.

Save these your servants:
free them from evil and the tyranny of the enemy.
Keep far from them the spirit of wickedness,
   falsehood, and greed.

Receive them into your kingdom
and open their hearts to understand your Gospel,
so that, as children of the light,
they may become members of your Church,
bear witness to your truth,
and put into practice your commands of love.

We ask this through Christ our Lord.

R. Amen.

D   Lord Jesus Christ,
when you climbed the mountain to preach,
you turned your disciples from the paths of sin
and revealed to them the beatitudes of your kingdom.

Help these your servants, who hear the word of the Gospel,
and protect them from the spirit of greed, of lust, and of pride.
May they find the blessings of your kingdom
in poverty and in hunger,
in mercy and in purity of heart.
May they work for peace and joyfully endure persecution
and so come to share your kingdom
and experience the mercy you promised.
May they finally see God in the joy of heaven
where you live and reign for ever and ever.

R. Amen.

E   O God,
Creator and Saviour of all,
in your love you have formed these your servants;
in your mercy you have called them and received them.

Probe their hearts today
and watch over them as they look forward to the coming
    of your Son.

Keep them in your providence
and complete in them the plan of your love.
Through their loyalty to Christ
may they be counted among his disciples on earth
and be acknowledged by him in heaven.

We ask this through Christ our Lord.

R. Amen.

F   Lord and God,
you know the secrets of our hearts
and reward us for the good we do.

Look kindly on the efforts and the progress of your servants.
Strengthen them on their way,
increase their faith,
and accept their repentance.

Open to them your goodness and justice
and lead them to share in your sacraments on earth,
until they finally enjoy your presence in heaven.

We ask this through Christ our Lord.

R. Amen.

G   Lord Jesus Christ,   373:1
     loving Redeemer of all,
     your name alone has the power to save,
     that name before which every knee should bend
     in the heavens, on the earth, and under the earth.

     We pray for these your servants,
     who worship you as the true God.

     Look upon them and enlighten their hearts,
     free them from the snares and malice of Satan,
     heal their weakness and blot out their sins.

     Give them discernment to know what pleases you
     and the courage to live by your Gospel,
     that they may become the dwelling place of your Spirit,
     for you live and reign for ever and ever.

     R. Amen.

H   Lord Jesus Christ,   373:2
     sent by the Father and anointed by the Spirit,
     when you read in the synagogue at Nazareth
     you fulfiled the words of the prophet Isaiah
     that proclaimed liberty to captives
     and announced a season of forgiveness.

     We pray for these your servants
     who have opened their ears and hearts to your word.
     Grant that they may grasp your moment of grace.

     Do not let their minds be troubled
     or their lives tied to earthly desires.
     Do not let them remain
     estranged from the hope of your promises
     or enslaved by a spirit of unbelief.
     Rather, let them believe in you,
     whom the Father has established as universal Lord
     and to whom he has subjected all things.

Let them submit themselves to the Spirit of grace,
so that, with hope in their calling,
they may join the priestly people
and share in the abundant joy of the new Jerusalem,
where you live and reign for ever and ever.

R. Amen.

I   Lord Jesus Christ,
after calming the storms and freeing the possessed,
you gave us a sign of your mercy
by calling Matthew, the tax collector, to follow you.
You chose him to record for all time
your command to teach all nations.

We pray for these your servants
who confess that they are sinners.

Hold in check the power of the evil one,
and show them your mercy;
heal in them the wounds of sin
and fill their hearts with your peace.

May they delight in their discovery of the Gospel
and generously follow your call,
for you live and reign for ever and ever.

R. Amen.

J   God of infinite wisdom,
you chose the apostle Paul
to proclaim your Son to every nation.

We pray that these your servants,
who look forward to baptism,
may follow in the footsteps of Paul
and trust not in flesh and blood,
but in the call of your grace.

Probe their hearts and purify them,
so that, freed from all deception,
they may never look back
but strive always toward what is to come.

May they count everything as loss
compared with the unsurpassed worth of knowing your Son,
and so gain him as their eternal reward,
for he is Lord for ever and ever.

R. Amen.

K   Lord,   373:5
Creator and Redeemer of your holy people,
your great love has drawn these catechumens
   to seek and find you.
Look upon them today,
purify their hearts,
and bring to fulfilment in them the plan of your grace,
so that, faithfully following Christ,
they may come to drink the waters of salvation.

We ask this through Christ our Lord.

R. Amen.

BLESSINGS OF THE CATECHUMENS

95   The blessings of the catechumens are a sign of God's love and of the
Church's tender care. They are bestowed on the catechumens so that, even
though they do not as yet have the grace of the sacraments, they may still
receive from the Church courage, joy, and peace as they proceed along
the difficult journey they have begun.

96   The blessings may be given by a priest, a deacon, or a qualified catechist appointed by the bishop (see no. 16). The blessings are usually given
at the end of a celebration of the word; they may also be given at the end
of a meeting for catechesis. When there is some special need, the blessings
may be given privately to individual catechumens.

PRAYERS OF BLESSING

97   The celebrant, with hands outstretched over the catechumens, says one of the following prayers. After the prayer of blessing, if this can be done conveniently, the catechumens come
before the celebrant, who lays hands on them individually. Then
the catechumens leave.

Let us pray.

A   Lord,
form these catechumens by the mysteries of the faith,
that they may be brought to rebirth in baptism
and be counted among the members of your Church.

We ask this through Christ our Lord.

R. Amen.

B   Father,
through your holy prophets
you proclaimed to all who draw near you,
'Wash and be cleansed,'
and through Christ you have granted us rebirth in the Spirit.

Bless these your servants
as they earnestly prepare for baptism.

Fulfil your promise:
sanctify them in preparation for your gifts,
that they may come to be reborn as your children
and enter the community of your Church.

We ask this through Christ our Lord.

R. Amen.

C   God of power,   123
look upon these your servants
as they deepen their understanding of the Gospel.

Grant that they may come to know and love you
and always heed your will
with receptive minds and generous hearts.

Teach them through this time of preparation
and enfold them within your Church,
so that they may share your holy mysteries
both on earth and in heaven.

We ask this through Christ our Lord.

R. Amen.

D   God our Father,   124
you have sent your only Son, Jesus Christ,
to free the world from falsehood.

Give to your catechumens fulness of understanding,
unwavering faith,
and a firm grasp of your truth.

Let them grow ever stronger,
that they may receive in due time the new birth of baptism
that gives pardon of sins,
and join with us in praising your name.

We ask this through Christ our Lord.

R. Amen.

E Almighty and eternal God,
you dwell on high yet look on the lowly;
to bring us your gift of salvation
you sent Jesus your Son,
our Lord and God.

Look kindly on these catechumens,
who bow before you in worship;
prepare them for their rebirth in baptism,
the forgiveness of their sins,
and the garment of incorruptible life.

Enfold them in your holy, catholic, and apostolic Church,
that they may join with us
in giving glory to your name.

We ask this through Christ our Lord.

R. Amen.

F Lord of all,
through your only begotten Son
you cast down Satan
and broke the chains that held us captive.

We thank you for these catechumens
whom you have called.

Strengthen them in faith,
that they may know you, the one true God,
and Jesus Christ, whom you have sent.

Keep them clean of heart and make them grow in virtue,
that they may be worthy to receive baptism
and enter into the holy mysteries.

We ask this through Christ our Lord.

R. Amen.

G   Lord God,   374:3
     you desire that all be saved
     and come to the knowledge of truth.

     Enliven with faith those who are preparing for baptism;
     bring them into the fold of your Church,
     there to receive the gift of eternal life.

     We ask this through Christ our Lord.

     R. Amen.

H   God of power and Father of our Saviour Jesus Christ,   374:4
     look kindly upon these your servants.

     Drive from their minds all taint of false worship
     and stamp your law and commands on their hearts.

     Lead them to full knowledge of the truth
     and prepare them to be the temple of the Holy Spirit
     through their rebirth in baptism.

     Grant this through Christ our Lord.

     R. Amen.

I   Lord,   374:5
     look with love on your servants,
     who commit themselves to your name
     and bow before you in worship.

     Help them to accomplish what is good;
     arouse their hearts,
     that they may always remember your works and your commands
     and eagerly embrace all that is yours.

     Grant this through Christ our Lord.

     R. Amen.

OPTIONAL RITES DURING THE CATECHUMENATE

ANOINTING OF THE CATECHUMENS

98   During the period of the catechumenate, a rite of anointing the catechumens, through use of the oil of catechumens, may be celebrated wherever this seems beneficial or desirable. The presiding celebrant for such a first anointing of the catechumens is a priest or a deacon.

99   The anointing ordinarily takes place after the homily in a celebration of the word of God (see no. 89), and is conferred on each of the catechumens; this rite of anointing may be celebrated several times during the course of the catechumenate. Further, for particular reasons, a priest or a deacon may confer the anointing privately on individual catechumens.

100 The oil used for this rite is to be the oil blessed by the bishop at the chrism Mass, but for pastoral reasons a priest celebrant may bless oil for the rite immediately before the anointing.[1]

Prayer of Exorcism or Blessing of Oil

101 When anointing with oil already blessed by the bishop, the celebrant first says the prayer of exorcism given as option A (or one of the other prayers of exorcism in no. 94); a priest celebrant who for pastoral reasons chooses to bless oil for the rite uses the blessing given as option B.

A   Prayer of Exorcism

Let us pray.

Lord Jesus Christ,
sent by the Father and anointed by the Spirit,
when you read in the synagogue at Nazareth,
you fulfilled the words of the prophet Isaiah
that proclaimed liberty to captives
and announced a season of forgiveness.

---

[1] See *Rite of the Blessing of Oils, Rite of Consecrating the Chrism,* Introduction, no. 7.

We pray for these your servants
who have opened their ears and hearts to your word.
Grant that they may grasp your moment of grace.

Do not let their minds be troubled
or their lives tied to earthly desires.
Do not let them remain
estranged from the hope of your promises
or enslaved by a spirit of unbelief.
Rather, let them believe in you,
whom the Father has established as universal Lord
and to whom he has subjected all things.

Let them submit themselves to the Spirit of grace,
so that, with hope in their calling,
they may join the priestly people
and share in the abundant joy of the new Jerusalem,
where you live and reign for ever and ever.

R. Amen.

B   BLESSING OF OIL

Let us pray.

O God,   131
source of strength and defender of your people,
you have chosen to make this oil,
created by your hand,
an effective sign of your power.

Bless ✠ this oil
and strengthen the catechumens who will be anointed with it.
Grant them your wisdom to understand the Gospel more deeply
and your strength to accept the challenges of Christian life.

Enable them to rejoice in baptism
and to partake of a new life in the Church
as true children of your family.

We ask this through Christ our Lord.

R. Amen.

102 Facing the catechumens, the celebrant says:

**We anoint you with the oil of salvation
in the name of Christ our Saviour.
May he strengthen you with his power,
who lives and reigns for ever and ever.**

Catechumens:

Amen.

The celebrant anoints each catechumen with the oil of catechumens on the breast or on both hands or, if this seems desirable, even on other parts of the body.

[If there are a great many catechumens, additional priests or deacons may assist in the anointing.]

The anointing may be followed by a blessing of the catechumens (no. 97).

PRESENTATIONS

103 The presentations normally take place during Lent, the period of purification and enlightenment, after the first and third scrutinies. But for pastoral advantage and because the period of purification and enlightenment is rather short, the presentations may be held during the period of the catechumenate, rather than at the regular times. But the presentations are not to take place until a point during the catechumenate when the catechumens are judged ready for these celebrations.

104 Both the presentation of the Creed and the presentation of the Lord's Prayer may be anticipated; each may be concluded with the ephphetha rite.[1] When the presentations are anticipated, care is to be taken to substitute the term 'catechumens' for the term 'elect' in all formularies.

PRESENTATIONS

Presentation of the Creed: see nos. 144-149.

Presentation of the Lord's Prayer: see nos. 165-170.

Ephphetha Rite: see nos. 184-186.

---

[1] But if the rite of recitation of the Creed (nos. 180-183) is also anticipated as one of the 'rites of passage' (see no. 33,6), the ephphetha rite is used only to begin this rite of recitation and not with the presentations.

SECOND STEP: ELECTION OR ENROLMENT OF NAMES

Your ways, O Lord, are love and truth to those who keep your covenant

105 The second step in Christian initiation is the liturgical rite called both election and the enrolment of names, which closes the period of the catechumenate proper, that is, the lengthy period of formation of the catechumens' minds and hearts. The celebration of the rite of election, which usually coincides with the opening of Lent, also marks the beginning of the period of final, more intense preparation for the sacraments of initiation, during which the elect will be encouraged to follow Christ with greater generosity. 134

106 At this second step, on the basis of the testimony of godparents and catechists and of the catechumens' reaffirmation of their intention, the Church judges their state of readiness and decides on their advancement toward the sacraments of initiation. Thus the Church makes its 'election,' that is, the choice and admission of those catechumens who have the dispositions that make them fit to take part, at the next major celebration, in the sacraments of initiation. 22 133

This step is called election because the acceptance made by the Church is founded on the election by God, in whose name the Church acts. The step is also called the enrolment of names because as a pledge of fidelity the candidates inscribe their names in the book that lists those who have been chosen for initiation.

107 Before the rite of election is celebrated, the catechumens are expected to have undergone a conversion in mind and in action and to have developed a sufficient acquaintance with Christian teaching as well as a spirit of faith and charity. With deliberate will and an enlightened faith they must have the intention to receive the sacraments of the Church, a resolve they will express publicly in the actual celebration of the rite. 23

108 The election, marked with a rite of such solemnity, is the focal point of the Church's concern for the catechumens. Admission to election therefore belongs to the bishop, and the presiding celebrant for the rite of election is the bishop himself or a priest or a deacon who acts as the bishop's delegate (see no. 12). 135

Before the rite of election the bishop, priests, deacons, catechists, godparents, and the entire community, in accord with their respective responsibilities and in their own way, should, after considering the matter carefully, arrive at a judgment about the catechumens' state of formation and progress. After the election, they should surround the elect with prayer, so that the entire Church will accompany and lead them to encounter Christ.

109 Within the rite of election the bishop celebrant or his delegate declares 23
13 in the presence of the community the Church's approval of the candidates. Therefore to exclude any semblance of mere formality from the rite, there should be a deliberation prior to its celebration to decide on the catechumens' suitableness. This deliberation is carried out by the priests, deacons, and catechists involved in the formation of the catechumens, and by the godparents and representatives of the local community. If circumstances suggest, the group of catechumens may also take part. The deliberation may take various forms, depending on local conditions and pastoral needs. During the celebration of election, the assembly is informed of the decision approving the catechumens.

110 Before the rite of election godparents are chosen by the catechumens; 13 the choice should be made with the consent of the priest, and the persons chosen should, as far as possible, be approved for their role by the local community (see no. 11). In the rite of election the godparents exercise their ministry publicly for the first time. They are called by name at the beginning of the rite to come forward with the catechumens (no. 117); they give testimony on behalf of the catechumens before the community (no. 118); they may also write their names along with the catechumens in the book of the elect (no. 119).

111 From the day of their election and admission, the catechumens are 24 called 'the elect.' They are also described as *competentes* ('co-petitioners'), because they are joined together in asking for and aspiring to receive the three sacraments of Christ and the gift of the Holy Spirit. They are also called *illuminandi* ('those who will be enlightened'), because baptism itself has been called *illuminatio* ('enlightenment') and it fills the newly baptised with the light of faith. In our own times, other names may be applied to the elect that, depending on regions and cultures, are better suited to the people's understanding and the idiom of the language.

112 The bishop celebrant or his delegate, however much or little he was 138 involved in the deliberation prior to the rite, has the responsibility of showing in the homily or elsewhere during the celebration the religious and ecclesial significance of the election. The celebrant also declares before all present the Church's decision and, if appropriate in the circumstances, asks the community to express its approval of the candidates. He also asks the catechumens to give a personal expression of their intention and, in the name of the Church, he carries out the act of admitting them as elect. The celebrant should open to all the divine mystery expressed in the call of the Church and in the liturgical celebration of this mystery. He should remind the faithful to give good example to the elect and along with the elect to prepare themselves for the Easter solemnities.

113 The sacraments of initiation are celebrated during the Easter solemnities, and preparation for these sacraments is part of the distinctive character of Lent. Accordingly, the rite of election should normally take place on the First Sunday of Lent and the period of final preparation of the elect should coincide with the Lenten season. The plan arranged for the Lenten season will benefit the elect by reason of both its liturgical structure and the participation of the community. For urgent pastoral reasons, especially in secondary mission stations, it is permitted to celebrate the rite of election during the week preceding or following the First Sunday of Lent.

When, because of unusual circumstances and pastoral needs, the rite of election is celebrated outside Lent, it is to be celebrated about six weeks before the sacraments of initiation, in order to allow sufficient time for the scrutinies and presentations. The rite is not to be celebrated on a solemnity of the liturgical year (see no. 29).

114 The rite should take place in the church or, if necessary, in some other suitable and fitting place.

115 The rite is celebrated within Mass, after the homily, and should be celebrated within the Mass of the First Sunday of Lent. If, for pastoral reasons, the rite is celebrated on a different day, the texts and the readings of the ritual Mass 'Christian Initiation: Election or Enrolment of Names' may always be used. When the Mass of the day is celebrated and its readings are not suitable, the readings are those given for the First Sunday of Lent or others may be chosen from elsewhere in the Lectionary.

When celebrated outside Mass, the rite takes place after the readings and the homily and is concluded with the dismissal of both the elect and the faithful.

OUTLINE OF THE RITE

LITURGY OF THE WORD

Homily
Presentation of the Catechumens
Affirmation by the Godparents [and the Assembly]
Invitation and Enrolment of Names
Act of Admission or Election
Intercessions for the Elect
Prayer over the Elect
Dismissal of the Elect

LITURGY OF THE EUCHARIST

RITE OF ELECTION OR ENROLMENT OF NAMES

LITURGY OF THE WORD

Homily

116 After the readings (see no. 115), the bishop, or the celebrant who acts as delegate of the bishop, gives the homily. This should be suited to the actual situation and should address not just the catechumens but the entire community of the faithful, so that all will be encouraged to give good example and to accompany the elect along the path of the paschal mystery.

142

Presentation of the Catechumens

117 After the homily, the priest in charge of the catechumens' initiation, or a deacon, a catechist, or a representative of the community, presents the candidates, using the following or similar words.

143

Reverend Father, Easter is drawing near, and so these catechumens, whom I now present to you, are completing their period of preparation. They have found strength in God's grace and support in our community's prayers and example.

Now they ask that after the celebration of the scrutinies, they be allowed to participate in the sacraments of baptism, confirmation, and the eucharist.

The celebrant replies:

Those who are to be chosen in Christ, come forward, together with your godparents.

One by one, the candidates and godparents are called by name. Each candidate, accompanied by a godparent (or godparents), comes forward and stands before the celebrant.

[If there are a great many candidates, all are presented in groups, for example, each group by its own catechist. But in this case, the catechists should be advised to have a special celebration beforehand in which they call each candidate forward by name.]

AFFIRMATION BY THE GODPARENTS [AND THE ASSEMBLY]

✗ 118 Then the celebrant addresses the assembly. If he has taken
part in the earlier deliberation on the candidates' suitableness
(see no. 109), he may use either option A or option B or similar
words; if he has not taken part in the earlier deliberation, he
uses option B or similar words.

A   My dear friends, these catechumens have asked to be initiated
into the sacramental life of the Church this Easter. Those who
know them have judged them to be sincere in their desire. During the period of their preparation they have listened to the word
of Christ and endeavoured to follow his commands; they have
shared the company of their Christian brothers and sisters and
joined with them in prayer.

And so I announce to all of you here that our community has
decided to call them to the sacraments. Therefore, I ask their
godparents to state their opinion once again, so that all of you
may hear.

He addresses the godparents:

As God is your witness, do you consider these candidates worthy to be admitted to the sacraments of Christian initiation?

Godparents:

We do.

[When appropriate in the circumstances, the celebrant may also
ask the entire assembly to express its approval of the candidates.]

B   God's holy Church wishes to know whether these candidates
are sufficiently prepared to be enrolled among the elect for the
coming celebration of Easter. And so I speak first of all to you
their godparents.

He addresses the godparents:

Have they faithfully listened to God's word proclaimed by the
Church?

Godparents:

They have.

Celebrant:

Have they responded to that word and begun to walk in God's presence?

Godparents:

They have.

Celebrant:

Have they shared the company of their Christian brothers and sisters and joined with them in prayer?

Godparents:

They have.

[When appropriate in the circumstances, the celebrant may also ask the entire assembly to express its approval of the candidates.]

Invitation and Enrolment of Names

119 Then addressing the catechumens in the following or similar words, the celebrant advises them of their acceptance and asks them to declare their own intention.

146

And now, my dear catechumens, I address you. Your own godparents and teachers [and this entire community] have spoken in your favour. The Church in the name of Christ accepts their judgment and calls you to the Easter sacraments.

Since you have already heard the call of Christ, you must now express your response to that call clearly and in the presence of the whole Church.

Therefore, do you wish to enter fully into the life of the Church through the sacraments of baptism, confirmation, and the eucharist?

Catechumens:

We do.

Celebrant:

Then offer your names for enrolment.

The candidates give their names, either going with their god-parents to the celebrant or while remaining in place, and the actual inscription of the names may be carried out in various ways. The candidates may inscribe their names themselves or they may call out their names, which are inscribed by the god-parents or by the minister who presented the candidates (see no. 117). As the enrolment is taking place, an appropriate song, for example, Psalm 15(16), may be sung.

[If there are a great many candidates, the enrolment may simply consist in the presentation of a list of the names to the celebrant, with such words as: 'These are the names of the candidates.']

ACT OF ADMISSION OR ELECTION

120 The celebrant briefly explains the significance of the enrol-ment that has just taken place. Then, turning to the candidates, he says the following or similar words.

N. and N., I now declare you to be members of the elect, to be initiated into the sacred mysteries at the next Easter Vigil.

Candidates:

Thanks be to God.

He continues:

God is always faithful to those he calls: now it is your duty, as it is ours, both to be faithful to him in return and to strive courageously to reach the fulness of truth, which your election opens up before you.

Then the celebrant turns to the godparents and instructs them in the following or similar words.

Godparents, you have spoken in favour of these catechumens: accept them now as chosen in the Lord and continue to sustain them through your loving care and example, until they come to share in the sacraments of God's life.

He invites them to place their hand on the shoulder of the can-didate whom they are receiving into their care, or to make some other gesture to indicate the same intent.

121 The community may use either of the following formular-ies, options A or B, or a similar formulary to pray for the elect. The celebrant may adapt the introduction and the intentions to fit various circumstances.

[If it is decided, in accord with no. 124, that after the dismissal of the elect the usual general intercessions of the Mass are to be omitted and that the liturgy of the eucharist is to begin im-mediately, intentions for the Church and the whole world are to be added to the following intentions for the elect.]

Celebrant:

My brothers and sisters, in beginning this period of Lent, we look forward to celebrating at Easter the life-giving mysteries of our Lord's suffering, death, and resurrection. These elect, whom we bring with us to the Easter sacraments, will look to us for an example of Christian renewal. Let us pray to the Lord for them and for ourselves, that we may be renewed by one another's efforts and together come to share the joys of Easter.

A   Assisting minister:

That together we may fruitfully employ this Lenten season to renew ourselves through self-denial and works of holiness, let us pray to the Lord:

R.   Lord, hear our prayer.

Assisting minister:

That our catechumens may always remember this day of their election and be grateful for the blessings they have received from heaven, let us pray to the Lord:

R.   Lord, hear our prayer.

Assisting minister:

That their teachers may always convey the beauty of God's word to those who search for it, let us pray to the Lord:

R.   Lord, hear our prayer.

Assisting minister:

That their godparents may be living examples of the Gospel, let us pray to the Lord:

R.   Lord, hear our prayer.

Assisting minister:

That their families, far from placing any obstacles in the way of these catechumens, may help them to follow the promptings of the Spirit, let us pray to the Lord:

R. Lord, hear our prayer.

Assisting minister:

That our community, during this Lenten period, may grow in charity and be constant in prayer, let us pray to the Lord:

R. Lord, hear our prayer.

Assisting minister:

That those who have not yet overcome their hesitation may trust in Christ and come to join our community as our brothers and sisters, let us pray to the Lord:

R. Lord, hear our prayer.

B

Assisting minister:

That these elect may find joy in daily prayer, we pray:

R. Lord, hear our prayer.

Assisting minister:

That, by praying to you often, they may grow ever closer to you, we pray:

R. Lord, hear our prayer.

Assisting minister:

That they may read your word and joyfully dwell on it in their hearts, we pray:

R. Lord, hear our prayer.

Assisting minister:

That they may humbly acknowledge their faults and work wholeheartedly to correct them, we pray:

R. Lord, hear our prayer.

Assisting minister:

That they may dedicate their daily work as a pleasing offering to you, we pray:

R. Lord, hear our prayer.

Assisting minister:

That each day of Lent they may do something in your honour,
we pray:

R. Lord, hear our prayer.

Assisting minister:

That they may abstain with courage from everything that defiles
the heart, we pray:

R. Lord, hear our prayer.

Assisting minister:

That they may grow to love and seek virtue and holiness of life,
we pray:

R. Lord, hear our prayer.

Assisting minister:

That they may renounce self and put others first, we pray:

R. Lord, hear our prayer.

Assisting minister:

That you will protect and bless their families, we pray:

R. Lord, hear our prayer.

Assisting minister:

That they may share with others the joy they have found in their
faith, we pray:

R. Lord, hear our prayer.

PRAYER OVER THE ELECT

122 After the intercessions, the celebrant, with hands outstretched over the elect, says one of the following prayers.

149

A Lord God,
you created the human race
and are the author of its renewal.
Bless all your adopted children
and add these chosen ones
to the harvest of your new covenant.

149

As true children of the promise,
may they rejoice in eternal life,
won, not by the power of nature,
but through the mystery of your grace.

We ask this through Christ our Lord.

R. Amen.

B   Father of love and power,   14
it is your will to establish everything in Christ
and to draw us into his all-embracing love.
Guide the elect of your Church:
strengthen them in their vocation,
build them into the kingdom of your Son,
and seal them with the Spirit of your promise.

We ask this through Christ our Lord.

R. Amen.

Dismissal of the Elect

123 If the eucharist is to be celebrated, the elect are normally   15
dismissed at this point by use of option A; if the elect are to stay
for the celebration of the eucharist, option B is used; if the eucharist is not to be celebrated, the entire assembly is dismissed
by use of option C.

A   The celebrant dismisses the elect in these or similar words.   15

My dear elect, you have set out with us on the road that leads
to the glory of Easter. Christ will be your way, your truth, and
your life. Until we meet again for the scrutinies, walk always
in his peace.

The elect:

Amen.

B   If for serious reasons the elect cannot leave (see no. 75,3) and   15
must remain with the baptised, they are to be instructed that
though they are present at the eucharist, they cannot take part
in it as the baptised do. They may be reminded of this by the
celebrant in these or similar words.

Although you cannot yet participate fully in the Lord's eucharist, stay with us as a sign of our hope that all God's children will eat and drink with the Lord and work with his Spirit to re-create the face of the earth.

C

The celebrant dismisses those present, using these or similar words.

Go in peace,
and may the Lord remain with you always.

All:

Thanks be to God.

An appropriate song may conclude the celebration.

LITURGY OF THE EUCHARIST

124 When the eucharist is to follow, intercessory prayer is resumed with the usual general intercessions for the needs of the Church and the whole world; then, if required, the profession of faith is said. But for pastoral reasons these general intercessions and the profession of faith may be omitted. The liturgy of the eucharist then begins as usual with the preparation of the gifts.

151

PERIOD OF PURIFICATION AND ENLIGHTENMENT

The water that I shall give will turn into a spring of eternal life

125 The period of purification and enlightenment, which the rite of elec- 21
tion begins, customarily coincides with Lent. In the liturgy and liturgical 152
catechesis of Lent the reminder of baptism already received or the preparation for its reception, as well as the theme of repentance, renew the entire community along with those being prepared to celebrate the paschal
mystery, in which each of the elect will share through the sacraments of
initiation.[1] For both the elect and the local community, therefore, the Lenten
season is a time for spiritual recollection in preparation for the celebration
of the paschal mystery.

126 This is a period of more intense spiritual preparation, consisting more 22
in interior reflection than in catechetical instruction, and is intended to 153
purify the minds and hearts of the elect as they search their own consciences
and do penance. This period is intended as well to enlighten the minds
and hearts of the elect with a deeper knowledge of Christ the Saviour. The
celebration of certain rites, particularly the scrutinies (see nos. 128-133)
and the presentations (see nos. 134-136), brings about this process of purification and enlightenment and extends it over the course of the entire Lent-
en season.

127 Holy Saturday is the day of proximate preparation for the celebra- 26
tion of the sacraments of initiation and on that day the rites of preparation
(see nos. 172-179) may be celebrated.

---

[1] See Vatican Council II, Decree on the Church's Missionary Activity *Ad gentes*, no. 14.

RITES BELONGING TO THE PERIOD OF PURIFICATION AND ENLIGHTENMENT

SCRUTINIES

128 The scrutinies, which are solemnly celebrated on Sundays and are reinforced by an exorcism, are rites for self-searching and repentance and have above all a spiritual purpose. The scrutinies are meant to uncover, then heal all that is weak, defective, or sinful in the hearts of the elect; to bring out, then strengthen all that is upright, strong, and good. For the scrutinies are celebrated in order to deliver the elect from the power of sin and Satan, to protect them against temptation, and to give them strength in Christ, who is the way, the truth, and the life. These rites, therefore, should complete the conversion of the elect and deepen their resolve to hold fast to Christ and to carry out their decision to love God above all.

129 Because they are asking for the three sacraments of initiation, the elect must have the intention of achieving an intimate knowledge of Christ and his Church, and they are expected particularly to progress in genuine self-knowledge through serious examination of their lives and true repentance.

130 In order to inspire in the elect a desire for purification and redemption by Christ, three scrutinies are celebrated. By this means, first of all, the elect are instructed gradually about the mystery of sin, from which the whole world and every person longs to be delivered and thus saved from its present and future consequences. Second, their spirit is filled with Christ the Redeemer, who is the living water (gospel of the Samaritan woman in the first scrutiny), the light of the world (gospel of the man born blind in the second scrutiny), the resurrection and the life (gospel of Lazarus in the third scrutiny). From the first to the final scrutiny the elect should progress in their perception of sin and their desire for salvation.

131 In the rite of exorcism (nos. 141, 155, 162), which is celebrated by a priest or a deacon, the elect, who have already learned from the Church as their mother the mystery of deliverance from sin by Christ, are freed from the effects of sin and from the influence of the devil. They receive new strength in the midst of their spiritual journey and they open their hearts to receive the gifts of the Saviour.

132 The priest or deacon who is the presiding celebrant should carry out the celebration in such a way that the faithful in the assembly will also derive benefit from the liturgy of the scrutinies and join in the intercessions for the elect.

133 The scrutinies should take place within the ritual Masses 'Christian Initiation: The Scrutinies,' which are celebrated on the Third, Fourth, and Fifth Sundays of Lent; the readings with their chants are those given for these Sundays in the Lectionary for Mass, Year A. When, for pastoral reasons, these ritual Masses cannot be celebrated on their proper Sundays, they are celebrated on other Sundays of Lent or even convenient days during the week.

When, because of unusual circumstances and pastoral needs, the period of purification and enlightenment takes place outside Lent, the scrutinies are celebrated on Sundays or even on weekdays, with the usual intervals between celebrations. They are not celebrated on solemnities of the liturgical year (see no. 30).

In every case the ritual Masses 'Christian Initiation: The Scrutinies' are celebrated and in this sequence: for the first scrutiny the Mass with the gospel of the Samaritan woman; for the second, the Mass with the gospel of the man born blind; for the third, the Mass with the gospel of Lazarus.

PRESENTATIONS

25
181

134 The presentations take place after the celebration of the scrutinies, unless, for pastoral reasons, they have been anticipated during the period of the catechumenate (see nos. 79, 103-104). Thus, with the catechumenal formation of the elect completed, the Church lovingly entrusts to them the Creed and the Lord's Prayer, the ancient texts that have always been regarded as expressing the heart of the Church's faith and prayer. These texts are presented in order to enlighten the elect. The Creed, as it recalls the wonderful deeds of God for the salvation of the human race, suffuses the vision of the elect with the sure light of faith. The Lord's Prayer fills them with a deeper realization of the new spirit of adoption by which they will call God their Father, especially in the midst of the eucharistic assembly.

183
184

135 The first presentation to the elect is the presentation of the Creed, during the week following the first scrutiny. The elect are to commit the Creed to memory and they will recite it publicly (nos. 180-183) prior to professing their faith in accordance with that Creed on the day of their baptism.

188
189

136 The second presentation to the elect is the presentation of the Lord's Prayer, during the week following the third scrutiny (but, if necessary, this presentation may be deferred for inclusion in the preparation rites of Holy Saturday; see no. 172). From antiquity the Lord's Prayer has been the prayer proper to those who in baptism have received the spirit of adoption. When the elect have been baptised and take part in their first celebration of the eucharist, they will join the rest of the faithful in saying the Lord's Prayer.

OUTLINE OF THE RITE

LITURGY OF THE WORD

Readings
Homily
Invitation to Silent Prayer
Intercessions for the Elect
Exorcism
Dismissal of the Elect

LITURGY OF THE EUCHARIST

FIRST SCRUTINY
(Third Sunday of Lent)

LITURGY OF THE WORD

READINGS

137 The texts and the readings for Mass are always those given for the first scrutiny in the Missal and the Lectionary for Mass among the ritual Masses, 'Christian Initiation: The Scrutinies' (Vol. III, p. 5, which simply cross-refers to Vol. I, pp. 245-250).

160

HOMILY

138 After the readings and guided by them, the celebrant explains in the homily the meaning of the first scrutiny in the light of the Lenten liturgy and of the spiritual journey of the elect.

161

INVITATION TO SILENT PRAYER

139 After the homily, the elect with their godparents come forward and stand before the celebrant.

162

The celebrant first addresses the assembly of the faithful, inviting them to pray in silence and to ask that the elect will be given a spirit of repentance, a sense of sin, and the true freedom of the children of God.

The celebrant then addresses the elect, inviting them also to pray in silence and suggesting that as a sign of their inner spirit of repentance they bow their heads or kneel; he concludes his remarks with the following or similar words.

Elect of God, bow your heads [kneel down] and pray.

The elect bow their heads or kneel, and all pray for some time in silence. After the period of silent prayer, the community and the elect stand for the intercessions.

INTERCESSIONS FOR THE ELECT

140 Either of the following formularies, options A or B, may be used for the intercessions for the elect and both the introduction and the intentions may be adapted to fit various circumstances. During the intercessions the godparents stand with their right hand on the shoulder of the elect.

[If it is decided, in accord with no. 143, that after the dismissal of the elect the usual general intercessions of the Mass are to be omitted and that the liturgy of the eucharist is to begin immediately, intentions for the Church and the whole world are to be added to the following intentions for the elect.]

Celebrant:

Let us pray for these elect whom the Church has confidently chosen. May they successfully complete their long preparation and at the paschal feast find Christ in his sacraments.

A   Assisting minister:

That they may ponder the word of God in their hearts and savour its meaning more fully day by day, let us pray to the Lord:

R.   **Lord, hear our prayer.**

Assisting minister:

That they may learn to know Christ, who came to save what was lost, let us pray to the Lord:

R.   **Lord, hear our prayer.**

Assisting minister:

That they may humbly confess themselves to be sinners, let us pray to the Lord:

R.   **Lord, hear our prayer.**

Assisting minister:

That they may sincerely reject everything in their lives that is displeasing and contrary to Christ, let us pray to the Lord:

R.   **Lord, hear our prayer.**

Assisting minister:

That the Holy Spirit, who searches every heart, may help them to overcome their weakness through his power, let us pray to the Lord:

R.   **Lord, hear our prayer.**

Assisting minister:

That the same Holy Spirit may teach them to know the things of God and how to please him, let us pray to the Lord:

R. Lord, hear our prayer.

Assisting minister:

That their families also may put their hope in Christ and find peace and holiness in him, let us pray to the Lord:

R. Lord, hear our prayer.

Assisting minister:

That we ourselves in preparation for the Easter feast may seek a change of heart, give ourselves to prayer, and persevere in our good works, let us pray to the Lord:

R. Lord, hear our prayer.

Assisting minister:

That throughout the whole world whatever is weak may be strengthened, whatever is broken restored, whatever is lost found, and what is found redeemed, let us pray to the Lord:

R. Lord, hear our prayer.

B   Assisting minister: 378

That, like the woman of Samaria, our elect may review their lives before Christ and acknowledge their sins, let us pray to the Lord:

R. Lord, hear our prayer.

Assisting minister:

That they may be freed from the spirit of mistrust that deters people from following Christ, let us pray to the Lord:

R. Lord, hear our prayer.

Assisting minister:

That while awaiting the gift of God, they may long with all their hearts for the living water that brings eternal life, let us pray to the Lord:

R. Lord, hear our prayer.

Assisting minister:

That by accepting the Son of God as their teacher, they may become true worshippers of the Father in spirit and in truth, let us pray to the Lord:

R. Lord, hear our prayer.

Assisting minister:

That they may share with their friends and neigbours the wonder of their own meeting with Christ, let us pray to the Lord:

R. Lord, hear our prayer.

Assisting minister:

That those whose lives are empty for want of the word of God may come to the Gospel of Christ, let us pray to the Lord:

R. Lord, hear our prayer.

Assisting minister:

That all of us may learn from Christ to do the Father's will in love, let us pray to the Lord:

R. Lord, hear our prayer.

EXORCISM

✗141 After the intercessions, the rite continues with one of the following exorcisms.

A The celebrant faces the elect and, with hands joined, says:

God of power,
you sent your Son to be our Saviour.
Grant that these catechumens,
who, like the woman of Samaria, thirst for living water,
may turn to the Lord as they hear his word
and acknowledge the sins and weaknesses
   that weigh them down.

Protect them from vain reliance on self
and defend them from the power of Satan.

Free them from the spirit of deceit,
so that, admitting the wrong they have done,
they may attain purity of heart
and advance on the way to salvation.

We ask this through Christ our Lord.

R. Amen.

Here, if this can be done conveniently, the celebrant lays hands on each one of the elect.

Then, with hands outstretched over all the elect, he continues:

Lord Jesus,
you are the fountain for which they thirst,
you are the Master whom they seek.
In your presence
they dare not claim to be without sin,
for you alone are the Holy One of God.

They open their hearts to you in faith,
they confess their faults
and lay bare their hidden wounds.
In your love free them from their infirmities,
heal their sickness,
quench their thirst, and give them peace.

In the power of your name,
which we call upon in faith,
stand by them now and heal them.
Rule over that spirit of evil,
conquered by your rising from the dead.

Show your elect the way of salvation in the Holy Spirit,
that they may come to worship the Father in truth,
for you live and reign for ever and ever.

R. Amen.

B

The celebrant faces the elect and, with hands joined, says: 379

All-merciful Father,
through your Son you revealed your mercy
to the woman of Samaria;
and moved by that same care
you have offered salvation to all sinners.

Look favourably on these elect,
who desire to become your adopted children
through the power of your sacraments.

Free them from the slavery of sin,
and for Satan's crushing yoke
exchange the gentle yoke of Jesus.

Protect them in every danger,
that they may serve you faithfully in peace and joy
and render you thanks for ever.

R. Amen.

Here, if this can be done conveniently, the celebrant lays hands on each one of the elect.

Then, with hands outstretched over all the elect, he continues:

Lord Jesus,
in your merciful wisdom
you touched the heart of the sinful woman
and taught her to worship the Father
in spirit and in truth.

Now, by your power,
free these elect from the cunning of Satan,
as they draw near to the fountain of living water.

Touch their hearts with the power of the Holy Spirit,
that they may come to know the Father
in true faith, which expresses itself in love,
for you live and reign for ever and ever.

R. Amen.

An appropriate song may be sung, for example, Psalm 6, 25(26), 31(32), 37(38), 38(39), 39(40), 50(51), 115(116):1-9, 129(130), 138(139), or 141(142).

DISMISSAL OF THE ELECT

142 If the eucharist is to be celebrated, the elect are normally dismissed at this point by use of option A; if the elect are to stay for the celebration of the eucharist, option B is used; if the eucharist is not to be celebrated, the entire assembly is dismissed by use of option C.

A   The celebrant dismisses the elect in these or similar words.

Dear elect, go in peace,
and join us again at the next scrutiny.
May the Lord remain with you always.

Elect:
Amen.

B   If for serious reasons the elect cannot leave (see no. 75,3) and must remain with the baptised, they are to be instructed that though they are present at the eucharist, they cannot take part in it as the baptised do. They may be reminded of this by the celebrant in these or similar words.

Although you cannot yet participate fully in the Lord's eucharist, stay with us as a sign of our hope that all God's children will eat and drink with the Lord and work with his Spirit to re-create the face of the earth.

C   The celebrant dismisses those present, using these or similar words.

Go in peace,
and may the Lord remain with you always.

All:
Thanks be to God.

An appropriate song may conclude the celebration.

LITURGY OF THE EUCHARIST

143 When the eucharist is to follow, intercessory prayer is resumed with the usual general intercessions for the needs of the Church and the whole world; then, if required, the profession of faith is said. But for pastoral reasons these general intercessions and the profession of faith may be omitted. The liturgy of the eucharist then begins as usual with the preparation of the gifts. In the eucharistic prayer there is to be a remembrance of the elect and their godparents (see ritual Mass 'Christian Initiation: The Scrutinies').

166

OUTLINE OF THE RITE

LITURGY OF THE WORD

Readings
Homily
Presentation of the Creed
Prayer over the Elect
Dismissal of the Elect

LITURGY OF THE EUCHARIST

PRESENTATION OF THE CREED
(Third Week of Lent)

182
184

144 The presentation of the Creed, which takes place during the week after the first scrutiny, should preferably be celebrated in the presence of a community of the faithful, within Mass after the homily.

LITURGY OF THE WORD

READINGS

185

145 In place of the readings assigned for the weekday Mass, the following readings are used, as indicated in the Lectionary for Mass, ritual Masses, 'Christian Initiation: Presentation of the Creed' (Vol. III, pp. 6-10).

FIRST READING
Deuteronomy 6:1-7 — *Listen, Israel: You shall love the Lord with all your heart.*

RESPONSORIAL PSALM
Psalm 18(19):8, 9, 10, 11
R. (John 6:68c) **You have the message of eternal life, O Lord.**

SECOND READING
Romans 10:8-13 — *The believer in God professes his faith.*
Or:
1 Corinthians 15:1-8a (longer) or 1-4 (shorter) — *The Gospel will save you only if you keep believing exactly what I preached to you.*

VERSE BEFORE THE GOSPEL
John 3:16
God loved the world so much,
that he gave his only Son;
everyone who believes in him
has eternal life.

GOSPEL
Matthew 16:13-18 — *On this rock I will build my Church.*
Or:
John 12:44-50 — *I, the light, have come into the world, so that whoever believes in me need not stay in the dark.*

HOMILY

185

146 After the readings and guided by them, the celebrant explains in the homily the meaning and importance of the Creed in relation to the teaching that the elect have already received and to the profession of faith that they must make at their baptism and uphold throughout their lives.

147 After the homily, a deacon or other assisting minister says:

Let the elect now come forward to receive the Creed from the Church.

Before beginning the Apostles' Creed (option A) or the Nicene Creed (option B), the celebrant addresses the elect in these or similar words.

My dear friends, listen carefully to the words of that faith by which you will be justified. The words are few, but the mysteries they contain are great. Receive them with a sincere heart and be faithful to them.

A   APOSTLES' CREED

The celebrant alone begins:

I believe in God, the Father almighty,

As the elect listen, he continues with the assembly of the faithful.

creator of heaven and earth.

I believe in Jesus Christ, his only Son, our Lord.
   He was conceived by the power of the Holy Spirit
      and born of the Virgin Mary.
   He suffered under Pontius Pilate,
      was crucified, died, and was buried.
   He descended to the dead.
   On the third day he rose again.
   He ascended into heaven,
      and is seated at the right hand of the Father.
   He will come again to judge the living and the dead.

I believe in the Holy Spirit,
   the holy catholic Church,
   the communion of saints,
   the forgiveness of sins,
   the resurrection of the body,
   and the life everlasting. Amen.

The celebrant alone begins:

We believe in one God,

As the elect listen, he continues with the assembly of the faithful.

the Father, the Almighty,
maker of heaven and earth,
of all that is, seen and unseen.

We believe in one Lord, Jesus Christ,
the only Son of God,
eternally begotten of the Father,
God from God, Light from Light,
true God from true God,
begotten, not made,
of one Being with the Father.
Through him all things were made.
For us men and for our salvation
he came down from heaven:
by the power of the Holy Spirit
he became incarnate from the Virgin Mary,
and was made man.
For our sake he was crucified under Pontius Pilate;
he suffered death and was buried.
On the third day he rose again
in accordance with the Scriptures;
he ascended into heaven
and is seated at the right hand of the Father.
He will come again in glory to judge the living and the dead,
and his kingdom will have no end.

We believe in the Holy Spirit, the Lord, the giver of life,
who proceeds from the Father and the Son.
With the Father and the Son he is worshipped and glorified.
He has spoken through the Prophets.
We believe in one holy catholic and apostolic Church.
We acknowledge one baptism for the forgiveness of sins.
We look for the resurrection of the dead,
and the life of the world to come. Amen.

PRAYER OVER THE ELECT

148 Using the following or similar words, the celebrant invites the faithful to pray.

Let us pray for these elect, that God in his mercy may make them responsive to his love, so that through the waters of rebirth they may receive pardon for their sins and have life in Christ Jesus our Lord.

All pray in silence.

Then the celebrant, with hands outstretched over the elect, says:

Lord,
eternal source of light, justice, and truth,
take under your tender care
your servants N. and N.

Purify them and make them holy;
give them true knowledge, sure hope, and sound understanding,
and make them worthy
to receive the grace of baptism.

We ask this through Christ our Lord.

R. Amen.

DISMISSAL OF THE ELECT

149 If the eucharist is to be celebrated, the elect are normally dismissed at this point by use of option A; if the elect are to stay for the celebration of the eucharist, option B is used; if the eucharist is not to be celebrated, the entire assembly is dismissed by use of option C.

A   The celebrant dismisses the elect in these or similar words.

Dear elect, go in peace,
and may the Lord remain with you always.

Elect:

Amen.

B If for serious reasons the elect cannot leave (see no. 75,3) and must remain with the baptised, they are to be instructed that though they are present at the eucharist, they cannot take part in it as the baptised do. They may be reminded of this by the celebrant in these or similar words.

Although you cannot yet participate fully in the Lord's eucharist, stay with us as a sign of our hope that all God's children will eat and drink with the Lord and work with his Spirit to re-create the face of the earth.

C The celebrant dismisses those present, using these or similar words.

**Go in peace,
and may the Lord remain with you always.**

All:
Thanks be to God.

An appropriate song may conclude the celebration.

LITURGY OF THE EUCHARIST

150 After the elect leave, the celebration of Mass continues in the usual way.

OUTLINE OF THE RITE

LITURGY OF THE WORD

Readings
Homily
Invitation to Silent Prayer
Intercessions for the Elect
Exorcism
Dismissal of the Elect

LITURGY OF THE EUCHARIST

SECOND SCRUTINY
(Fourth Sunday of Lent)

LITURGY OF THE WORD

READINGS

151 The texts and readings for Mass are always those given for the second scrutiny in the Missal and the Lectionary for Mass among the ritual Masses, 'Christian Initiation: The Scrutinies' (Vol. III, p. 5, which simply cross-refers to Vol. I, pp. 276-280, and offers an alternative First Reading (Exodus 13:21-22). 167

HOMILY

152 After the readings and guided by them, the celebrant explains in the homily the meaning of the second scrutiny in the light of the Lenten liturgy and of the spiritual journey of the elect. 168

INVITATION TO SILENT PRAYER

153 After the homily, the elect with their godparents come forward and stand before the celebrant. 169

The celebrant first addresses the assembly of the faithful, inviting them to pray in silence and to ask that the elect will be given a spirit of repentance, a sense of sin, and the true freedom of the children of God.

The celebrant then addresses the elect, inviting them also to pray in silence and suggesting that as a sign of their inner spirit of repentance they bow their heads or kneel; he concludes his remarks with the following or similar words.

Elect of God, bow your heads [kneel down] and pray.

The elect bow their heads or kneel, and all pray for some time in silence. After the period of silent prayer, the community and the elect stand for the intercessions.

154 Either of the following formularies, options A or B, may be used for the intercessions for the elect and both the introduction and the intentions may be adapted to fit various circumstances. During the intercessions the godparents stand with their right hand on the shoulder of the elect.

[If it is decided, in accord with no. 157, that after the dismissal of the elect the usual general intercessions of the Mass are to be omitted and that the liturgy of the eucharist is to begin immediately, intentions for the Church and the whole world are to be added to the following intentions for the elect.]

Celebrant:

Let us pray for these elect whom God has called, that they may remain faithful to him and boldly give witness to the words of eternal life.

A   Assisting minister:

That, trusting in the truth of Christ, they may find freedom of mind and heart and preserve it always, let us pray to the Lord:

R. Lord, hear our prayer.

Assisting minister:

That, preferring the folly of the cross to the wisdom of the world, they may glory in God alone, let us pray to the Lord:

R. Lord, hear our prayer.

Assisting minister:

That, freed by the power of the Spirit, they may put all fear behind them and press forward with confidence, let us pray to the Lord:

R. Lord, hear our prayer.

Assisting minister:

That, transformed in the Spirit, they may seek those things that are holy and just, let us pray to the Lord:

R. Lord, hear our prayer.

Assisting minister:

That all who suffer persecution for Christ's name may find their strength in him, let us pray to the Lord:

R. Lord, hear our prayer.

Assisting minister:

That those families and nations prevented from embracing the faith may be granted freedom to believe the Gospel, let us pray to the Lord:

R. Lord, hear our prayer.

Assisting minister:

That we who are faced with the values of the world may remain faithful to the spirit of the Gospel, let us pray to the Lord:

R. Lord, hear our prayer.

Assisting minister:

That the whole world, which the Father so loves, may attain in the Church complete spiritual freedom, let us pray to the Lord:

R. Lord, hear our prayer.

B Assisting minister: 382

That God may dispel darkness and be the light that shines in the hearts of our elect, let us pray to the Lord:

R. Lord, hear our prayer.

Assisting minister:

That he may gently lead them to Christ, the light of the world, let us pray to the Lord:

R. Lord, hear our prayer.

Assisting minister:

That our elect may open their hearts to God and acknowledge him as the source of light and the witness of truth, let us pray to the Lord:

R. Lord, hear our prayer.

Assisting minister:

That he may heal them and preserve them from the unbelief of this world, let us pray to the Lord:

R. Lord, hear our prayer.

Assisting minister:

That, saved by him who takes away the sin of the world, they may be freed from the contagion and forces of sin, let us pray to the Lord:

R. Lord, hear our prayer.

That, enlightened by the Holy Spirit, they may never fail to profess the Good News of salvation and share it with others, let us pray to the Lord:

R. Lord, hear our prayer.

Assisting minister:

That all of us, by the example of our lives, may become in Christ the light of the world, let us pray to the Lord:

R. Lord, hear our prayer.

Assisting minister:

That every inhabitant of the earth may acknowledge the true God, the Creator of all things, who bestows upon us the gift of Spirit and life, let us pray to the Lord:

R. Lord, hear our prayer.

EXORCISM

155 After the intercessions, the rite continues with one of the following exorcisms.

17

A   The celebrant faces the elect and, with hands joined, says: 17

Father of mercy,
you led the man born blind
to the kingdom of light
through the gift of faith in your Son.

Free these elect
from the false values that surround and blind them.
Set them firmly in your truth,
children of the light for ever.

We ask this through Christ our Lord.

R. Amen.

Here, if this can be done conveniently, the celebrant lays hands on each one of the elect.

Then, with hands outstretched over all the elect, he continues:

Lord Jesus,
you are the true light that enlightens the world.
Through your Spirit of truth
free those who are enslaved by the father of lies.

Stir up the desire for good in these elect,
whom you have chosen for your sacraments.

Let them rejoice in your light, that they may see,
and, like the man born blind whose sight you restored,
let them prove to be staunch and fearless witnesses to the faith,
for you are Lord for ever and ever.

R. Amen.

B The celebrant faces the elect and, with hands joined, says: 383

Lord God,
source of unfailing light,
by the death and resurrection of Christ
you have cast out the darkness of hatred and lies
and poured forth the light of truth and love
upon the human family.

Hear our prayers for these elect,
whom you have called to be your adopted children.

Enable them to pass from darkness to light
and, delivered from the prince of darkness,
to live always as children of the light.

We ask this through Christ our Lord.

R. Amen.

Here, if this can be done conveniently, the celebrant lays hands on each one of the elect.

Then, with hands outstretched over all the elect, he continues:

Lord Jesus,
at your own baptism
the heavens were opened
and you received the Holy Spirit
to empower you to proclaim the Good News to the poor
and restore sight to the blind.

Pour out the same Holy Spirit on these elect,
who long for your sacraments.
Guide them along the paths of right faith,
safe from error, doubt, and unbelief,
so that with eyes unsealed
they may come to see you face to face,
for you live and reign for ever and ever.

R. Amen.

An appropriate song may be sung, for example, Psalm 6, 25(26),
31(32), 37(38), 38(39), 39(40), 50(51), 115(116):1-9, 129(130),
138(139), or 141(142).

DISMISSAL OF THE ELECT

156 If the eucharist is to be celebrated, the elect are normally
dismissed at this point by use of option A; if the elect are to stay
for the celebration of the eucharist, option B is used; if the eucharist is not to be celebrated, the entire assembly is dismissed
by use of option C.

A   The celebrant dismisses the elect in these or similar words.

Dear elect, go in peace,
and join us again at the next scrutiny.
May the Lord remain with you always.

Elect:

Amen.

B   If for serious reasons the elect cannot leave (see no. 75,3) and
must remain with the baptised, they are to be instructed that
though they are present at the eucharist, they cannot take part
in it as the baptised do. They may be reminded of this by the
celebrant in these or similar words.

Although you cannot yet participate fully in the Lord's eucharist, stay with us as a sign of our hope that all God's children will eat and drink with the Lord and work with his Spirit to re-create the face of the earth.

C   The celebrant dismisses those present, using these or similar words.

Go in peace,
and may the Lord remain with you always.

    All:

Thanks be to God.

An appropriate song may conclude the celebration.

LITURGY OF THE EUCHARIST

When the eucharist is to follow, intercessory prayer is resumed with the usual general intercessions for the needs of the Church and the whole world; then, if required, the profession of faith is said. But for pastoral reasons these general intercessions and the profession of faith may be omitted. The liturgy of the eucharist then begins as usual with the preparation of the gifts. In the eucharistic prayer there is to be a remembrance of the elect and their godparents (see ritual Mass 'Christian Initiation: The Scrutinies'). 173

OUTLINE OF THE RITE

LITURGY OF THE WORD

Readings
Homily
Invitation to Silent Prayer
Intercessions for the Elect
Exorcism
Dismissal of the Elect

LITURGY OF THE EUCHARIST

THIRD SCRUTINY
(Fifth Sunday of Lent)

LITURGY OF THE WORD

READINGS

158 The texts and readings for Mass are always those given for
the third scrutiny in the Missal and the Lectionary for Mass
among the ritual Masses, 'Christian Initiation: The Scrutinies'
(Vol. III, p. 5, which simply cross-refers to Vol. I, pp. 305-309).

174

HOMILY

159 After the readings and guided by them, the celebrant explains in the homily the meaning of the third scrutiny in the light
of the Lenten liturgy and of the spiritual journey of the elect.

175

INVITATION TO SILENT PRAYER

160 After the homily, the elect with their godparents come forward and stand before the celebrant.

176

The celebrant first addresses the assembly of the faithful, inviting them to pray in silence and to ask that the elect will be given
a spirit of repentance, a sense of sin, and the true freedom of
the children of God.

The celebrant then addresses the elect, inviting them also to pray
in silence and suggesting that as a sign of their inner spirit of
repentance they bow their heads or kneel; he concludes his remarks with the following or similar words.

Elect of God, bow your heads [kneel down] and pray.

The elect bow their heads or kneel, and all pray for some time
in silence. After the period of silent prayer, the community and
the elect stand for the intercessions.

Intercessions for the Elect

161 Either of the following formularies, options A or B, may be used for the intercessions for the elect and both the introduction and the intentions may be adapted to fit various circumstances. During the intercessions the godparents stand with their right hand on the shoulder of the elect.

[If it is decided, in accord with no. 164, that after the dismissal of the elect the usual general intercessions of the Mass are to be omitted and that the liturgy of the eucharist is to begin immediately, intentions for the Church and the whole world are to be added to the following intentions for the elect.]

Celebrant:

Let us pray for these elect whom God has chosen. May the grace of the sacraments conform them to Christ in his passion and resurrection and enable them to triumph over the bitter fate of death.

A

Assisting minister:

That faith may strengthen them against worldly deceits of every kind, let us pray to the Lord:

R. **Lord, hear our prayer.**

Assisting minister:

That they may always thank God, who has chosen to rescue them from their ignorance of eternal life and to set them on the way of salvation, let us pray to the Lord:

R. **Lord, hear our prayer.**

Assisting minister:

That the example and prayers of catechumens who have shed their blood for Christ may encourage these elect in their hope of eternal life, let us pray to the Lord:

R. **Lord, hear our prayer.**

Assisting minister:

That they may all have a horror of sin, which distorts life, let us pray to the Lord:

R. **Lord, hear our prayer.**

Assisting minister:

That those who are saddened by the death of family or friends may find comfort in Christ, let us pray to the Lord:

℟. Lord, hear our prayer.

Assisting minister:

That we too at Easter may again be confirmed in our hope of rising to life with Christ, let us pray to the Lord:

℟. Lord, hear our prayer.

Assisting minister:

That the whole world, which God has created in love, may flower in faith and charity and so receive new life, let us pray to the Lord:

℟. Lord, hear our prayer.

B   *Assisting minister:*   386

That these elect may be given the faith to acknowledge Christ as the resurrection and the life, we pray to the Lord:

℟. Lord, hear our prayer.

Assisting minister:

That they may be freed from sin and grow in the holiness that leads to eternal life, we pray to the Lord:

℟. Lord, hear our prayer.

Assisting minister:

That liberated by repentance from the shackles of sin they may become like Christ by baptism, dead to sin and alive for ever in God's sight, we pray to the Lord:

℟. Lord, hear our prayer.

Assisting minister:

That they may be filled with the hope of the life-giving Spirit and prepare themselves thoroughly for their birth to new life, we pray to the Lord:

℟. Lord, hear our prayer.

Assisting minister:

That the eucharistic food, which they are soon to receive, may make them one with Christ, the source of life and of resurrection, we pray to the Lord:

R. Lord, hear our prayer.

Assisting minister:

That all of us may walk in newness of life and show to the world the power of the risen Christ, we pray to the Lord:

R. Lord, hear our prayer.

Assisting minister:

That all the world may find Christ and acknowledge in him the promises of eternal life, we pray to the Lord:

R. Lord, hear our prayer.

EXORCISM

162 After the intercessions, the rite continues with one of the following exorcisms.

A   The celebrant faces the elect and, with hands joined, says:

Father of life and God not of the dead but of the living,
you sent your Son to proclaim life,
to snatch us from the realm of death,
and to lead us to the resurrection.

Free these elect
from the death-dealing power of the spirit of evil,
so that they may bear witness
to their new life in the risen Christ,
for he lives and reigns for ever and ever.

R. Amen.

Here, if this can be done conveniently, the celebrant lays hands on each one of the elect.

Then, with hands outstretched over all the elect, he continues:

Lord Jesus,
by raising Lazarus from the dead
you showed that you came that we might have life
and have it more abundantly.

Free from the grasp of death
those who await your life-giving sacraments
and deliver them from the spirit of corruption.

Through your Spirit, who gives life,
fill them with faith, hope, and charity,
that they may live with you always
in the glory of your resurrection,
for you are Lord for ever and ever.

R. Amen.

B   The celebrant faces the elect and, with hands joined, says: 387

Father,
source of all life,
in giving life to the living you seek out the image of your glory
and in raising the dead you reveal your unbounded power.

Rescue these elect from the tyranny of death,
for they long for new life through baptism.

Free them from the slavery of Satan,
the source of sin and death,
who seeks to corrupt the world you created
and saw to be good.

Place them under the reign of your beloved Son,
that they may share in the power of his resurrection
and give witness to your glory before all.

We ask this through Christ our Lord.

R. Amen.

Here, if this can be done conveniently, the celebrant lays hands on each one of the elect.

Then, with hands outstretched over all the elect, he continues:

Lord Jesus Christ,
you commanded Lazarus to step forth alive from his tomb
and by your own resurrection freed all people from death.

We pray for these your servants,
who eagerly approach the waters of new birth
and hunger for the banquet of life.

Do not let the power of death hold them back,
for, by their faith,
they will share in the triumph of your resurrection,
for you live and reign for ever and ever.

R. Amen.

An appropriate song may be sung, for example, Psalm 6, 25(26), 31(32), 37(38), 38(39), 39(40), 50(51), 115(116):1-9, 129(130), 138(139), or 141(142).

Dismissal of the Elect

163 If the eucharist is to be celebrated, the elect are normally dismissed at this point by use of option A; if the elect are to stay for the celebration of the eucharist, option B is used; if the eucharist is not to be celebrated, the entire assembly is dismissed by use of option C.

A   The celebrant dismisses the elect in these or similar words.

Dear elect, go in peace,
and may the Lord remain with you always.

Elect:
Amen.

B   If for serious reasons the elect cannot leave (see no. 75,3) and must remain with the baptised, they are to be instructed that though they are present at the eucharist, they cannot take part in it as the baptised do. They may be reminded of this by the celebrant in these or similar words.

Although you cannot yet participate fully in the Lord's eucharist, stay with us as a sign of our hope that all God's children will eat and drink with the Lord and work with his Spirit to re-create the face of the earth.

C   The celebrant dismisses those present, using these or similar words.

Go in peace,
and may the Lord remain with you always.

   All:
Thanks be to God.

An appropriate song may conclude the celebration.

LITURGY OF THE EUCHARIST

164 When the eucharist is to follow, intercessory prayer is resumed with the usual general intercessions for the needs of the Church and the whole world; then, if required, the profession of faith is said. But for pastoral reasons these general intercessions and the profession of faith may be omitted. The liturgy of the eucharist then begins as usual with the preparation of the gifts. In the eucharistic prayer there is to be a remembrance of the elect and their godparents (see ritual Mass 'Christian Initiation: The Scrutinies').

180

OUTLINE OF THE RITE

LITURGY OF THE WORD

Readings
Gospel Reading (Presentation of the Lord's Prayer)
Homily
Prayer over the Elect
Dismissal of the Elect

LITURGY OF THE EUCHARIST

PRESENTATION OF THE LORD'S PRAYER
(Fifth Week of Lent)

182
189

165 The presentation of the Lord's Prayer, which takes place during the week after the third scrutiny, should preferably be celebrated in the presence of a community of the faithful, within Mass.

LITURGY OF THE WORD

READINGS

190

166 In place of the first reading assigned for the weekday Mass, the following two readings are used, as indicated in the Lectionary for Mass, ritual Masses, 'Christian Initiation: Presentation of the Lord's Prayer' (Vol. III, pp. 10-13).

FIRST READING

Hosea 11:1b, 3-4, 8c-9 — *I led them with leading-strings of love.*

RESPONSORIAL PSALM

Psalm 22(23):1-3a, 3b-4, 5, 6

R. (v.1) **The Lord is my shepherd;**
there is nothing I shall want.

Or:

Psalm 102(103):1-2, 8 and 10, 11-12, 13 and 18

R. (v.3) **As a father has compassion on his sons,**
the Lord has pity on those who fear him.

SECOND READING

Romans 8:14-17, 26-27 — *The spirit you received is the spirit of sons, and it makes us cry out, 'Abba, Father!'*

Or:

Galatians 4:4-7 — *God has sent the spirit of his Son into our hearts: the Spirit that cries, 'Abba, Father!'*

VERSE BEFORE THE GOSPEL

Romans 8:15

The spirit you received is the spirit of sons,
and it makes us cry out, 'Abba, Father!'

Gospel Reading (Presentation of the Lord's Prayer)

167 After the first and second reading, an assisting deacon or other minister says:

Let those who are to receive the Lord's Prayer now come forward.

The celebrant first addresses the following or similar words to the elect.

Listen to the gospel reading in which our Lord teaches his followers how to pray.

The gospel reading follows, with the version of the Lord's Prayer, options A or B, in use in the region.

A reading from the holy gospel according to Saint Matthew.

At that time Jesus said to his disciples:
'Say this when you pray:

A   "Our Father,
who art in heaven,
hallowed be thy name;
thy kingdom come;
thy will be done on earth
as it is in heaven.
Give us this day our daily bread
and forgive us our trespasses
as we forgive those
who trespass against us;
and lead us not into temptation,
but deliver us from evil."'

B   "Our Father in heaven,
hallowed be your Name,
your kingdom come,
your will be done,
on earth as in heaven.
Give us today our daily bread.
Forgive us our sins
as we forgive those who sin against us.
Save us from the time of trial
and deliver us from evil."'

Homily

191

168 After the gospel presentation, the celebrant in the homily explains the meaning and importance of the Lord's Prayer.

Prayer over the Elect

192

169 After the homily, the celebrant, using the following or similar words, invites the faithful to pray.

Let us pray for these elect, that God in his mercy may make them responsive to his love, so that through the waters of rebirth they may receive pardon for their sins and have life in Christ Jesus our Lord.

All pray in silence.

Then the celebrant, with hands outstretched over the elect, says:

Almighty and eternal God,
you continually enlarge the family of your Church.

Deepen the faith and understanding
of these elect, chosen for baptism.
Give them new birth in your living waters,
so that they may be numbered among your adopted children.

We ask this through Christ our Lord.

℟. Amen.

Dismissal of the Elect

170 If the eucharist is to be celebrated, the elect are normally dismissed at this point by use of option A; if the elect are to stay for the celebration of the eucharist, option B is used; if the eucharist is not to be celebrated, the entire assembly is dismissed by use of option C.

A   The celebrant dismisses the elect in these or similar words.

Dear elect, go in peace,
and may the Lord remain with you always.

Elect:

Amen.

B　　　If for serious reasons the elect cannot leave (see no. 75,3) and must remain with the baptised, they are to be instructed that though they are present at the eucharist, they cannot take part in it as the baptised do. They may be reminded of this by the celebrant in these or similar words.

Although you cannot yet participate fully in the Lord's eucharist, stay with us as a sign of our hope that all God's children will eat and drink with the Lord and work with his Spirit to re-create the face of the earth.

C　　　The celebrant dismisses those present, using these or similar words.

Go in peace,
and may the Lord remain with you always.

All:
Thanks be to God.

An appropriate song may conclude the celebration.

LITURGY OF THE EUCHARIST

171 After the elect leave, the celebration of Mass continues in the usual way.

PREPARATION RITES
ON HOLY SATURDAY

172 In proximate preparation for the celebration of the sacraments of initiation: _{26 193}

    1. The elect are to be advised that on Holy Saturday they should refrain from their usual activities, spend their time in prayer and reflection, and, as far as they can, observe a fast.

    2. When it is possible to bring the elect together on Holy Saturday for reflection and prayer, some or all of the following rites may be celebrated as an immediate preparation for the sacraments: the presentation of the Lord's Prayer, if it has been deferred (see nos. 136, 165-167), the 'return' or recitation of the Creed (nos. 180-183), the ephphetha rite (nos. 184-186), the choosing of a baptismal name (nos. 187-189), and the anointing with the oil of catechumens (nos. 190-194; for the rite of anointing the celebrant is a priest or deacon).

173 The choice and arrangement of these rites should be guided by what best suits the particular circumstances of the elect, but the following should be observed with regard to their celebration: _{195 197 206}

    1. In cases where celebration of the presentation of the Creed was not possible, the recitation of the Creed is not celebrated.

    2. When both the recitation of the Creed and the ephphetha rite are celebrated, the ephphetha rite immediately precedes the 'Prayer before the Recitation' (no. 182).

    3. When included as a preparatory rite, the anointing with the oil of catechumens (nos. 190-194), which may be celebrated separately, may also be combined with the recitation of the Creed, either beforehand to prepare for the recitation or afterward to reinforce it.

174 SONG: When the elect have gathered, the celebration begins with a suitable song.

175 GREETING: After the singing, the celebrant greets the elect and any of the faithful who are present, using one of the greetings for Mass or other suitable words.

176 READING OF THE WORD OF GOD: Where indicated in the particular rites, the reading of the word of God follows; the readings may be chosen from those suggested for each rite. If more than one reading is used, a suitable psalm or hymn may be sung between the readings.

177 HOMILY: Where indicated in the particular rites, a brief homily or an explanation of the text follows the reading of the word of God.

178 CELEBRATION OF THE RITES CHOSEN: See nos. 180-194.

179 CONCLUDING RITES: The celebration may be concluded with the prayer of blessing and dismissal given in nos. 196-197.

RECITATION OF THE CREED

180 The rite of recitation of the Creed prepares the elect for the profes- 194
sion of faith they will make immediately before they are baptised (no. 219);
the rite also instructs them in their duty to proclaim the message of the
Gospel.

READING AND HOMILY

181 One of the following readings (Lectionary, Vol. III, pp. 14-15) 196
may be used, or another appropriate reading may be chosen.

Matthew 16:13-17 — *You are the Christ, the Son of the living God.*
Or:
John 6:35, 63-71 — *Lord, who shall we go to? You have the message of eternal life*

A brief homily follows.

[If the ephphetha rite (nos. 184-186) is to be included as a preparation rite, it is celebrated before the following prayer.]

PRAYER BEFORE THE RECITATION

182 The celebrant, with hands outstretched, says the following 198
prayer.

Let us pray.

Lord,
we pray to you for these elect,
who have now accepted for themselves
the loving purpose and the mysteries
that you revealed in the life of your Son.

As they profess their belief with their lips,
may they have faith in their hearts
and accomplish your will in their lives.

We ask this through Christ our Lord.

R. Amen.

RECITATION OF THE CREED

183 The elect then recite the Creed. Depending on the version that was entrusted to them at the presentation, they recite either the Apostles' Creed, option A, or the Nicene Creed, option B.

A   APOSTLES' CREED

Elect:

I believe in God, the Father almighty,
    creator of heaven and earth.

I believe in Jesus Christ, his only Son, our Lord.
    He was conceived by the power of the Holy Spirit
        and born of the Virgin Mary.
    He suffered under Pontius Pilate,
        was crucified, died, and was buried.
    He descended to the dead.
    On the third day he rose again.
    He ascended into heaven,
        and is seated at the right hand of the Father.
    He will come again to judge the living and the dead.

I believe in the Holy Spirit,
    the holy catholic Church,
    the communion of saints,
    the forgiveness of sins,
    the resurrection of the body,
    and the life everlasting. Amen.

B   NICENE CREED

Elect:

We believe in one God,
    the Father, the Almighty,
    maker of heaven and earth,
    of all that is, seen and unseen.

We believe in one Lord, Jesus Christ,
　　the only Son of God,
　　eternally begotten of the Father,
　　God from God, Light from Light,
　　true God from true God,
　　begotten, not made,
　　of one Being with the Father.
　　Through him all things were made.
　　For us men and for our salvation
　　　　he came down from heaven:
　　by the power of the Holy Spirit
　　　　he became incarnate from the Virgin Mary,
　　　　　　and was made man.
　　For our sake he was crucified under Pontius Pilate;
　　　　he suffered death and was buried.
　　　　On the third day he rose again
　　　　　　in accordance with the Scriptures;
　　　　he ascended into heaven
　　　　　　and is seated at the right hand of the Father.
　　He will come again in glory to judge the living and the dead,
　　　　and his kingdom will have no end.

We believe in the Holy Spirit, the Lord, the giver of life,
　　who proceeds from the Father and the Son.
　　With the Father and the Son he is worshipped and glorified.
　　He has spoken through the Prophets.
　　We believe in one holy catholic and apostolic Church.
　　We acknowledge one baptism for the forgiveness of sins.
　　We look for the resurrection of the dead,
　　　　and the life of the world to come. Amen.

EPHPHETHA RITE

184 By the power of its symbolism the ephphetha rite, or rite of opening the ears and mouth, impresses on the elect their need of grace in order that they may hear the word of God and profess it for their salvation.

READING AND INSTRUCTION

185 The reading is as indicated for this rite in the Lectionary for Mass (Vol. III, p. 15); the celebrant gives a brief explanation of the text.

Mark 7:31-37 —'Ephphetha', that is, 'Be opened.'

EPHPHETHA

186 The elect come before the celebrant. A suitable song may be sung as the celebrant touches the right and left ear and the closed lips of each of the elect with his thumb and says the following formulary.

[If there are a great many elect, additional priests or deacons may assist in carrying out the rite.]

Ephphetha: that is, be opened,
that you may profess the faith you hear,
to the praise and glory of God.

CHOOSING A BAPTISMAL NAME

187 The rite of choosing a baptismal name may be celebrated on Holy Saturday, unless it was included in the rite of acceptance into the order of catechumens (see no. 73). The elect may choose a new name, which is either a traditional Christian name or a name of regional usage that is not incompatible with Christian beliefs. Where it seems better suited to the circumstances and the elect are not too numerous, the naming may consist simply in an explanation of the given name of each of the elect.

READING AND INSTRUCTION

188 There may be a reading — chosen, for example, from the following list (Lectionary, Vol. III, pp. 15-17) — and a brief explanation by the celebrant.

1   Genesis 17:1-7 — *You will be called Abraham.*
2   Isaiah 62:1-5 — *You will be called by a new name.*
3   Apocalypse 3:11-13 — *I will inscribe on them my own new name.*
4   Matthew 16:13-18 — *You are Peter.*
5   John 1:40-42 — *You are to be called Peter.*

NAMING OF THE ELECT

189 If as baptismal names the elect have chosen new names, option A is used; if they are to use their given names, option B is used.

A   The celebrant asks each of the elect to state the new name chosen; then he says the following or similar words.

N., from now on you will [also] be called N.

The elect responds by saying 'Amen' or in some other suitable way.

B   The celebrant applies some Christian interpretation to the given name of each of the elect.

ANOINTING WITH THE OIL OF CATECHUMENS

190 If the conference of bishops has not decided on its omission altogether
(see no. 33,7), the anointing with the oil of catechumens that ordinarily
forms part of the liturgy of baptism (no. 218) may be anticipated on Holy
Saturday to save time in the celebration of the Easter Vigil. The presiding
celebrant is a priest or a deacon.

191 When this anointing is anticipated, care is to be taken that the elect
who are to be baptised understand its significance. The anointing with oil
symbolizes their need for God's help and strength so that, undeterred by
the bonds of the past and overcoming the opposition of the devil, they will
forthrightly take the step of professing their faith and will hold fast to it
unfalteringly throughout their lives.

192 The oil used for this rite is to be the oil blessed by the bishop at the
chrism Mass, but for pastoral reasons a priest celebrant may bless oil for
the rite immediately before the anointing.

BLESSING OF OIL

193 A priest celebrant who for pastoral reasons chooses to bless
oil for the rite uses the following prayer of blessing.

O God,
source of strength and defender of your people,
you have chosen to make this oil,
created by your hand,
an effective sign of your power.

Bless ✠ this oil
and strengthen the catechumens who will be anointed with it.
Grant them your wisdom to understand the Gospel more deeply
and your strength to accept the challenges of Christian life.

Enable them to rejoice in baptism
and to partake of a new life in the Church
as true children of your family.

We ask this through Christ our Lord.

R. Amen.

---

194 The celebrant, facing the elect, says:

**We anoint you with the oil of salvation
in the name of Christ our Saviour.
May he strengthen you with his power,
who lives and reigns for ever and ever.**

Elect:

Amen.

The celebrant anoints each one of the elect with the oil of catechumens on the breast or on both hands, or if this seems desirable, even on other parts of the body.

[If there are a great many elect, additional priests or deacons may assist in the anointing.]

During the anointing an appropriate song may be sung.

CONCLUDING RITES

195 The celebration of the preparation rites may be concluded with a prayer of blessing over the elect and a dismissal.

PRAYER OF BLESSING

196 The celebrant invites those present to pray.

Let us pray.

Then, with hands outstretched over the elect, the celebrant says the following prayer.

Father,
through your holy prophets
you proclaimed to all who draw near you,
'Wash and be cleansed,'
and through Christ you have granted us rebirth in the Spirit.

Bless these your servants
as they earnestly prepare for baptism.

Fulfil your promise:
sanctify them in preparation for your gifts,
that they may come to be reborn as your children
and enter the community of your Church.

We ask this through Christ our Lord.

R. **Amen.**

DISMISSAL

197 The celebrant may inform the elect of the time and place they are to meet for the Easter Vigil; the celebrant then dismisses them, using the following or another suitable formulary.

May the Lord be with you
until we gather again
to celebrate his paschal mystery.

Elect:

Amen.

THIRD STEP: CELEBRATION OF THE SACRAMENTS OF INITIATION

When we were baptised we joined Jesus in death
so that we might walk in the newness of his life

198 The third step in the Christian initiation of adults is the celebration of the sacraments of baptism, confirmation, and eucharist. Through this final step the elect, receiving pardon for their sins, are admitted into the people of God. They are graced with adoption as children of God and are led by the Holy Spirit into the promised fulness of time begun in Christ[1] and, as they share in the eucharistic sacrifice and meal, even to a foretaste of the kingdom of God.

199 The usual time for the celebration of the sacraments of initiation is the Easter Vigil (see no. 23), at which preferably the bishop himself presides as celebrant, at least for the initiation of those who are fourteen years old or older (see no. 12). As indicated in the Roman Missal, 'Easter Vigil' (no. 44), the conferral of the sacraments follows the blessing of the water.

200 When the celebration takes place outside the usual time (see nos. 26-27), care should be taken to ensure that it has a markedly paschal character (see *Christian Initiation*, General Introduction, no. 6). Thus the texts for one of the ritual Masses 'Christian Initiation: Baptism' given in the Roman Missal are used, and the readings are chosen from those given in the Lectionary for Mass, 'Celebration of the Sacraments of Initiation apart from the Easter Vigil.'

CELEBRATION OF BAPTISM

201 The celebration of baptism has as its centre and high point the baptismal washing and the invocation of the Holy Trinity. Beforehand there are rites that have an inherent relationship to the baptismal washing: first, the blessing of water, then the renunciation of sin by the elect, their anointing with the oil of catechumens, and their profession of faith. Following the baptismal washing, the effects received through this sacrament are given expression in the explanatory rites: the anointing with chrism (when confirmation does not immediately follow baptism), the clothing with a white garment, and the presentation of a lighted candle.

---

[1] See Vatican Council II, Dogmatic Constitution on the Church *Lumen gentium*, no. 48; also Ephesians 1:10.

202 PRAYER OVER THE WATER: The celebration of baptism begins with the blessing of water, even when the sacraments of initiation are received outside the Easter season. Should the sacraments be celebrated outside the Easter Vigil but during the Easter season (see no. 26), the water blessed at the Vigil is used, but a prayer of thanksgiving, having the same themes as the blessing, is included. The blessing declares the religious meaning of water as God's creation and the sacramental use of water in the unfolding of the paschal mystery, and the blessing is also a remembrance of God's wonderful works in the history of salvation.

The blessing thus introduces an invocation of the Trinity at the very outset of the celebration of baptism. For it calls to mind the mystery of God's love from the beginning of the world and the creation of the human race; by invoking the Holy Spirit and proclaiming Christ's death and resurrection, it impresses on the mind the newness of Christian baptism, by which we share in his own death and resurrection and receive the holiness of God himself.

203 RENUNCIATION OF SIN AND PROFESSION OF FAITH: In their renunciation of sin and profession of faith those to be baptised express their explicit faith in the paschal mystery that has already been recalled in the blessing of water and that will be connoted by the words of the sacrament soon to be spoken by the baptising minister. Adults are not saved unless they come forward of their own accord and with the will to accept God's gift through their own belief. The faith of those to be baptised is not simply the faith of the Church, but the personal faith of each one of them and each one of them is expected to keep it a living faith.

Therefore the renunciation of sin and the profession of faith are an apt prelude to baptism, the sacrament of that faith by which the elect hold fast to God and receive new birth from him. Because of the renunciation of sin and the profession of faith, which form the one rite, the elect will not be baptised merely passively but will receive this great sacrament with the active resolve to renounce error and to hold fast to God. By their own personal act in the rite of renouncing sin and professing their faith, the elect, as was prefigured in the first covenant with the patriarchs, renounce sin and Satan in order to commit themselves for ever to the promise of the Saviour and to the mystery of the Trinity. By professing their faith before the celebrant and the entire community, the elect express the intention, developed to maturity during the preceding periods of initiation, to enter into a new covenant with Christ. Thus these adults embrace the faith that through divine help the Church has handed down, and are baptised in that faith.

204 ANOINTING WITH THE OIL OF CATECHUMENS: The anointing with the oil of catechumens takes place between the renunciation and the profes-

sion of faith, unless this anointing has been anticipated in the preparation rites of Holy Saturday (see no. 190) or the conference of bishops has decreed its omission from the baptismal rites (see no. 33,7). This anointing symbolizes the need of the elect for God's help and strength so that, undeterred by the bonds of the past and overcoming the opposition of the devil, they will forthrightly take the step of professing their faith and will hold fast to it unfalteringly throughout their lives.

205 BAPTISM: Immediately after their profession of living faith in Christ's paschal mystery, the elect come forward and receive that mystery as expressed in the washing with water; thus once the elect have professed faith in the Father, Son, and Holy Spirit, invoked by the celebrant, the divine persons act so that those they have chosen receive divine adoption and become members of the people of God. [31]

206 Therefore in the celebration of baptism the washing with water should take on its full importance as the sign of that mystical sharing in Christ's death and resurrection through which those who believe in his name die to sin and rise to eternal life. Either immersion or the pouring of water should be chosen for the rite, whichever will serve in individual cases and in the various traditions and circumstances to ensure the clear understanding that this washing is not a mere purification rite but the sacrament of being joined to Christ. [32]

207 EXPLANATORY RITES: The baptismal washing is followed by rites that give expression to the effects of the sacrament just received. The anointing with chrism is a sign of the royal priesthood of the baptised and that they are now numbered in the company of the people of God. The clothing with the baptismal garment signifies the new dignity they have received. The presentation of a lighted candle shows that they are called to walk as befits the children of the light. [33]

CELEBRATION OF CONFIRMATION

208 In accord with the ancient practise followed in the Roman liturgy, adults are not to be baptised without receiving confirmation immediately afterward, unless some serious reason stands in the way. The conjunction of the two celebrations signifies the unity of the paschal mystery, the close link between the mission of the Son and the outpouring of the Holy Spirit, and the connection between the two sacraments through which the Son and the Holy Spirit come with the Father to those who are baptised. [34]

209 Accordingly, confirmation is conferred after the explanatory rites of baptism, the anointing after baptism (no. 222) being omitted. [35]

THE NEOPHYTES' FIRST SHARING IN THE CELEBRATION OF THE EUCHARIST

210 Finally in the celebration of the eucharist, as they take part for the first time and with full right, the newly baptised reach the culminating point in their Christian initiation. In this eucharist the neophytes, now raised to the ranks of the royal priesthood, have an active part in both the general intercessions and, to the extent possible, in bringing the gifts to the altar. With the entire community they share in the offering of the sacrifice and say the Lord's Prayer, giving expression to the spirit of adoption as God's children that they have received in baptism. When in communion they receive the body that was given for us and the blood that was shed, the neophytes are strengthened in the gifts they have already received and are given a foretaste of the eternal banquet.

OUTLINE OF THE RITE

SERVICE OF LIGHT

LITURGY OF THE WORD

CELEBRATION OF BAPTISM

Presentation of the Candidates
Invitation to Prayer
Litany of the Saints
Prayer over the Water
Profession of Faith
    Renunciation of Sin
    [Anointing with the Oil of Catechumens]
    Profession of Faith
Baptism
Explanatory Rites
    [Anointing after Baptism]
    [Clothing with a Baptismal Garment]
    Presentation of a Lighted Candle

CELEBRATION OF CONFIRMATION

Invitation
Laying on of Hands
Anointing with Chrism

LITURGY OF THE EUCHARIST

CELEBRATION OF THE SACRAMENTS OF INITIATION
(Easter Vigil)

CELEBRATION OF BAPTISM

213

211 The celebration of baptism begins after the homily. It takes place at the baptismal font, if this is in view of the faithful; otherwise in the sanctuary, where a vessel of water for the rite should be prepared beforehand.

PRESENTATION OF THE CANDIDATES

213

212 Accordingly, one of the following procedures, options A, B, or C, is chosen for the presentation of the candidates.

A   *When Baptism Is Celebrated Immediately at the Baptismal Font*
The celebrant accompanied by the assisting ministers goes directly to the font. An assisting deacon or other minister calls the candidates forward and their godparents present them. Then the candidates and the godparents take their place around the font in such a way as not to block the view of the congregation. The invitation to prayer (no. 213) and the Litany of the Saints (no. 214) follow.

[If there are a great many candidates, they and their godparents simply take their place around the font during the singing of the Litany of Saints.]

B   *When Baptism Is Celebrated after a Procession to the Font*
There may be a full procession to the baptismal font. In this case an assisting deacon or other minister calls the candidates forward and their godparents present them.

[If there are a great many candidates, they and their godparents simply take their place in the procession.]

The procession is formed in this order: a minister carries the Easter candle at the head of the procession (unless, outside the Easter Vigil, it already rests at the baptismal font), the candidates with their godparents come next, then the celebrant with the assisting ministers. The Litany of the Saints (no. 214) is sung during the procession. When the procession has reached the font, the candidates and their godparents take their place around the font in such a way as not to block the view of the congregation. The invitation to prayer (no. 213) precedes the blessing of the water.

C   *When Baptism Is Celebrated in the Sanctuary*
An assisting deacon or other minister calls the candidates forward and their godparents present them. The candidates and their godparents take their place before the celebrant in the sanctuary in such a way as not to block the view of the congregation. The invitation to prayer (no. 213) and the Litany of the Saints (no. 214) follow.

[If there are a great many candidates, they and their godparents simply take their place in the sanctuary during the singing of the Litany of the Saints.]

INVITATION TO PRAYER

213 The celebrant addresses the following or a similar invitation for the assembly to join in prayer for the candidates.

Dear friends, let us pray to almighty God for our brothers and sisters, N. and N., who are asking for baptism. He has called them and brought them to this moment; may he grant them light and strength to follow Christ with resolute hearts and to profess the faith of the Church. May he give them the new life of the Holy Spirit, whom we are about to call down on this water.

LITANY OF THE SAINTS

214 The singing of the Litany of the Saints is led by cantors and may include, at the proper place, names of other saints (for example, the titular of the church, the patron saints of the place or of those to be baptised) or petitions suitable to the occasion.

Lord, have mercy   Lord, have mercy
Christ, have mercy   Christ, have mercy
Lord, have mercy   Lord, have mercy

Holy Mary, Mother of God	pray for us
Saint Michael	pray for us
Holy Angels of God	pray for us
Saint John the Baptist	pray for us
Saint Joseph	pray for us
Saint Peter and Saint Paul	pray for us
Saint Andrew	pray for us
Saint John	pray for us
Saint Mary Magdalene	pray for us
Saint Stephen	pray for us
Saint Ignatius	pray for us
Saint Lawrence	pray for us
Saint Perpetua and Saint Felicity	pray for us
Saint Agnes	pray for us
Saint Gregory	pray for us
Saint Augustine	pray for us
Saint Athanasius	pray for us
Saint Basil	pray for us
Saint Martin	pray for us
Saint Benedict	pray for us
Saint Francis and Saint Dominic	pray for us
Saint Francis Xavier	pray for us
Saint John Vianney	pray for us
Saint Catherine	pray for us
Saint Teresa	pray for us
All holy men and women	pray for us

Lord, be merciful	Lord, save your people
From all evil	Lord, save your people
From every sin	Lord, save your people
From everlasting death	Lord, save your people
By your coming as man	Lord, save your people
By your death and rising to new life	Lord, save your people
By your gift of the Holy Spirit	Lord, save your people

Be merciful to us sinners	Lord, hear our prayer
Give new life to these chosen ones by the grace of baptism	Lord, hear our prayer
Jesus, Son of the living God	Lord, hear our prayer
Christ, hear us	Christ, hear us
Lord Jesus, hear our prayer	Lord Jesus, hear our prayer

215 After the Litany of the Saints, the celebrant blesses the water, using the blessing formulary given in option A.

When baptism is celebrated outside the Easter Vigil (see no. 26), the celebrant may use any of the blessing formularies given in options A, B, and C.

But when baptism is celebrated during the Easter season (see no. 26) and water already blessed at the Easter Vigil is available, the celebrant uses either option D or option E, so that this part of the celebration will retain the themes of thanksgiving and intercession.

A   BLESSING OF THE WATER: Facing the font (or vessel) containing the water, the celebrant sings the following (the text without music follows on p. 130).

Fa - ther, you give us grace through sac- ra-ment-al signs,

which tell us of the won - ders of your

un - seen power. In baptism we use your gift

of wa-ter, which you have made a rich sym - bol

of the grace you give us in this sac - ra - ment.

At the very dawn of creation your Spirit

breathed on the wa-ters, making them the well-spring

of all ho-li-ness. The waters of the great flood

you made a sign of the wa-ters of bap-tism

that make an end of sin and a new be-gin-ning

of good-ness. Through the waters of the Red Sea

you led Is-ra-el out of slav-ery to be an image of

God's ho-ly peo-ple, set free from sin_ by bap-tism.

In the waters of the Jor-dan your Son was

bap-tized by John and a-noint-ed with the Spir-it.

Your Son willed that water and blood should flow from

his side as he hung up-on the cross.

After his resurrection he told his dis-ci-ples:

"Go out and teach all nations, baptizing them in the name of the Father, and of the Son, and of the Holy Spirit." Father, look now with love upon your Church and unseal for it the fountain of baptism. By the power of the Holy Spirit give to this water the grace of your Son, so that in the sacrament of baptism all those whom you have created in your likeness may be cleansed from sin and rise to a new birth of innocence by water and the Holy Spirit.

Here, if this can be done conveniently, the celebrant before continuing lowers the Easter candle into the water once or three times, then holds it there until the acclamation at the end of the blessing.

[Outside the Easter Vigil, the celebrant before continuing simply touches the water with his right hand.]

We ask you, Fa-ther, with your Son to send the
Ho-ly Spir-it upon the waters of this font.
May all who are buried with Christ in the death
of bap-tism rise also with him to new-ness of life.
We ask this through Christ our Lord. ℟. A - men.

The people sing the following or some other suitable acclamation.

Springs of wa - ter, bless the Lord.
Give him glo - ry and praise for ev - er.

Father,
you give us grace through sacramental signs,
which tell us of the wonders of your unseen power.

In baptism we use your gift of water,
which you have made a rich symbol of the grace
you give us in this sacrament.

At the very dawn of creation
your Spirit breathed on the waters,
making them the wellspring of all holiness.

The waters of the great flood
you made a sign of the waters of baptism
that make an end of sin
and a new beginning of goodness.

Through the waters of the Red Sea
you led Israel out of slavery
to be an image of God's holy people,
set free from sin by baptism.

In the waters of the Jordan
your Son was baptised by John
and anointed with the Spirit.

Your Son willed that water and blood should flow from his side
as he hung upon the cross.

After his resurrection he told his disciples:
'Go out and teach all nations,
baptising them in the name of the Father, and of the Son,
    and of the Holy Spirit.'

Father,
look now with love upon your Church
and unseal for it the fountain of baptism.

By the power of the Holy Spirit
give to this water the grace of your Son,
so that in the sacrament of baptism
all those whom you have created in your likeness
may be cleansed from sin
and rise to a new birth of innocence
by water and the Holy Spirit.

Here, if this can be done conveniently, the celebrant before continuing lowers the Easter candle into the water once or three times, then holds it there until the acclamation at the end of the blessing.

[Outside the Easter Vigil, the celebrant before continuing simply touches the water with his right hand.]

**We ask you, Father, with your Son
to send the Holy Spirit upon the waters of this font.
May all who are buried with Christ in the death of baptism
rise also with him to newness of life.**

We ask this through Christ our Lord.

All:

Amen.

The people say the following or some other suitable acclamation.

**Springs of water, bless the Lord.
Give him glory and praise for ever.**

B   Blessing of Water: Facing the font (or vessel) containing the water, the celebrant says the following.

**Praise to you, almighty God and Father,
for you have created water to cleanse and to give life.**

389

All sing or say the following or some other suitable acclamation.

Blessed be God.

Celebrant:

**Praise to you, Lord Jesus Christ, the Father's only Son,
for you offered yourself on the cross,
that in the blood and water flowing from your side
and through your death and resurrection
the Church might be born.**

All:

Blessed be God.

Celebrant:

**Praise to you, God the Holy Spirit,
for you anointed Christ at his baptism in the waters
   of the Jordan,
that we might all be baptised in you.**

All:

Blessed be God.

Celebrant:

Come to us, Lord, Father of all,
and make holy this water which you have created,
so that all who are baptised in it may be washed clean of sin
and be born again to live as your children.

All sing or say the following or some other suitable invocation.

Hear us, Lord.

Celebrant:

Make this water holy, Lord,
so that all who are baptised into Christ's death
    and resurrection by this water
may become more perfectly like your Son.

All:

Hear us, Lord.

The celebrant touches the water with his right hand and continues.

Lord,
make holy this water which you have created,
so that all those whom you have chosen
may be born again by the power of the Holy Spirit
and may take their place among your holy people.

All:

Hear us, Lord.

C   BLESSING OF WATER: Facing the font (or vessel) containing the water, the celebrant says the following.

Father, God of mercy,
through these waters of baptism
you have filled us with new life as your very own children.

All sing or say the following or some other suitable acclamation.

Blessed be God.

Celebrant:

From all who are baptised in water and the Holy Spirit,
you have formed one people,
united in your Son, Jesus Christ.

All:

Blessed be God.

Celebrant:

You have set us free and filled our hearts with the Spirit
   of your love,
that we may live in your peace.

All:

Blessed be God.

Celebrant:

You call those who have been baptised
to announce the Good News of Jesus Christ
   to people everywhere.

All:

Blessed be God.

The celebrant concludes with the following.

You have called your children, N. and N.,
to this cleansing water and new birth,
that by sharing the faith of your Church
   they may have eternal life.
Bless ✠ this water in which they will be baptised.

We ask this in the name of Jesus the Lord.

All:

Amen.

D   EASTER-SEASON THANKSGIVING OVER WATER ALREADY BLESSED:
      Facing the font (or vessel) containing the blessed water, the cel-
      ebrant says the following.

Praise to you, almighty God and Father,   389
for you have created water to cleanse and to give life.

All sing or say the following or some other suitable acclamation.

Blessed be God.

Celebrant:

Praise to you, Lord Jesus Christ, the Father's only Son,
for you offered yourself on the cross,
that in the blood and water flowing from your side
and through your death and resurrection
the Church might be born.

All:

Blessed be God.

Celebrant:

Praise to you, God the Holy Spirit,
for you anointed Christ at his baptism in the waters
    of the Jordan,
that we might all be baptised in you.

All:

Blessed be God.

The celebrant concludes with the following prayer.

You have called your children, N. and N., to this cleansing water,
that they may share in the faith of your Church
    and have eternal life.
By the mystery of this consecrated water
lead them to a new and spiritual birth.

We ask this through Christ our Lord.

All:

Amen.

E   EASTER-SEASON THANKSGIVING OVER WATER ALREADY BLESSED:
    Facing the font (or vessel) containing the blessed water, the cel-
    ebrant says the following.

Father, God of mercy,
through these waters of baptism
you have filled us with new life as your very own children.

All sing or say a suitable acclamation or the following.
Blessed be God.

Celebrant:

From all who are baptised in water and the Holy Spirit,
you have formed one people,
united in your Son, Jesus Christ.

All:

Blessed be God.

Celebrant:

You have set us free and filled our hearts with the Spirit
    of your love,
that we may live in your peace.

All:

Blessed be God.

Celebrant:

You call those who have been baptised
to announce the Good News of Jesus Christ
    to people everywhere.

All:

Blessed be God.

The celebrant concludes with the following.

You have called your children, N. and N., to this cleansing water,
that they may share in the faith of your Church
    and have eternal life.
By the mystery of this consecrated water
lead them to a new and spiritual birth.

We ask this through Christ our Lord.

All:

Amen.

PROFESSION OF FAITH

216 After the blessing of the water (or prayer of thanksgiving),
the celebrant continues with the profession of faith, which includes the renunciation of sin and the profession itself (between
these there may be the anointing).

Renunciation of Sin

217 Using one of the following formularies, the celebrant questions all the elect together; or, after being informed of each candidate's name by the godparents, he may use the same formularies to question the candidates individually.

[If circumstances require, the conference of bishops may make the three formularies more specific and detailed, especially in regions where it is necessary for the candidates to reject superstitious and magical practises (see no. 72).]

A

Celebrant:

Do you reject sin so as to live in the freedom of God's children?

Candidates:

I do.

Celebrant:

**Do you reject the glamour of evil,
and refuse to be mastered by sin?**

Candidates:

I do.

Celebrant:

Do you reject Satan, father of sin and prince of darkness?

Candidates:

I do.

B

Celebrant:

**Do you reject Satan,
and all his works,
and all his empty promises?**

Candidates:

I do.

C

Celebrant:

Do you reject Satan?

Candidates:

I do.

Celebrant:
And all his works?

Candidates:
I do.

Celebrant:
And all his empty promises?

Candidates:
I do.

ANOINTING WITH THE OIL OF CATECHUMENS

218 Unless the conference of bishops has decided on its omission (see no. 33,7) or it has been anticipated as a preparation rite (nos. 190-194), the anointing with the oil of catechumens takes place between the renunciation and the profession of faith.

The celebrant says:
We anoint you with the oil of salvation in the name of Christ our Saviour. May he strengthen you with his power, who lives and reigns for ever and ever.

Candidates:
Amen.

The celebrant anoints each candidate with the oil of catechumens on both hands, on the breast, or, if this seems desirable, on other parts of the body.

[If there are a great many candidates, additional priests or deacons may assist in the anointing.]

PROFESSION OF FAITH

219 Then the celebrant, informed again of each candidate's name by the godparents, questions the candidates individually. Each candidate is baptised immediately after his or her profession of faith.

[If there are a great many to be baptised, the profession of faith
may be made simultaneously either by all together or group by
group, then the baptism of each candidate follows.]

Celebrant:

**N., do you believe in God, the Father almighty,
creator of heaven and earth?**

Candidate:

I do.

Celebrant:

**Do you believe in Jesus Christ, his only Son, our Lord,
who was born of the Virgin Mary,
was crucified, died, and was buried,
rose from the dead,
and is now seated at the right hand of the Father?**

Candidate:

I do.

Celebrant:

**Do you believe in the Holy Spirit,
the holy catholic Church, the communion of saints,
the forgiveness of sins, the resurrection of the body,
and the life everlasting?**

Candidate:

I do.

BAPTISM

220 The celebrant baptises each candidate either by immersion,
option A, or by the pouring of water, option B. Each baptism
may be followed by a short acclamation (Appendix, no. 452),
sung or said by the people.

[If there are a great number to be baptised, they may be divided
into groups and baptised by assisting priests or deacons. In baptising, either by immersion, option A, or by the pouring of water, option B, these ministers say the sacramental formulary for
each candidate. During the baptisms, singing by the people is
desirable or readings from Scripture or simply silent prayer.]

A   If baptism is by immersion, of the whole body or of the head 220
only, decency and decorum should be preserved. Either or both
godparents touch the candidate. The celebrant, immersing the
candidate's whole body or head three times, baptises the candidate in the name of the Trinity.

N., I baptise you in the name of the Father,

He immerses the candidate the first time.

and of the Son,

He immerses the candidate the second time.

and of the Holy Spirit.

He immerses the candidate the third time.

B   If baptism is by the pouring of water, either or both godparents 221
place the right hand on the shoulder of the candidate, and the
celebrant, taking baptismal water and pouring it three times on
the candidate's bowed head, baptises the candidate in the name
of the Trinity.

N., I baptise you in the name of the Father,

He pours water the first time.

and of the Son,

He pours water the second time.

and of the Holy Spirit.

He pours water the third time.

EXPLANATORY RITES

221 The celebration of baptism continues with the explanatory 223
rites, after which the celebration of confirmation normally follows.

ANOINTING AFTER BAPTISM

222 If the confirmation of those baptised is separated from their 224
baptism, the celebrant anoints them with chrism immediately
after baptism.

[When a great number have been baptised, assisting priests or
deacons may help with the anointing.]

The celebrant first says the following over all the newly baptised before the anointing.

**The God of power and Father of our Lord Jesus Christ
has freed you from sin
and brought you to new life
through water and the Holy Spirit.**

**He now anoints you with the chrism of salvation,
so that, united with his people,
you may remain for ever a member of Christ
who is Priest, Prophet, and King.**

Newly baptised:

Amen.

In silence each of the newly baptised is anointed with chrism on the crown of the head.

Clothing with a Baptismal Garment

223 The garment used in this rite may be white or of a colour that conforms to local custom. If circumstances suggest, this rite may be omitted.

The celebrant says the following formulary, and at the words 'Receive this baptismal garment' the godparents place the garment on the newly baptised.

**N. and N., you have become a new creation
and have clothed yourselves in Christ.
Receive this baptismal garment
and bring it unstained to the judgment seat
   of our Lord Jesus Christ,
so that you may have everlasting life.**

Newly baptised:

Amen.

224 The celebrant takes the Easter candle in his hands or touches it, saying to the godparents:

Godparents, please come forward to give to the newly baptised the light of Christ.

A godparent of each of the newly baptised goes to the celebrant, lights a candle from the Easter candle, then presents it to the newly baptised.

Then the celebrant says to the newly baptised:

You have been enlightened by Christ.
Walk always as children of the light
and keep the flame of faith alive in your hearts.
When the Lord comes, may you go out to meet him
with all the saints in the heavenly kingdom.

Newly baptised:

Amen.

[If the celebration of confirmation is to be deferred, the renewal of baptismal promises, as in the Roman Missal, 'Easter Vigil' (no. 46), now takes place; then the neophytes are led back to their places among the faithful.]

[Outside the Easter Vigil, if confirmation is to be deferred, the neophytes are led back to their places among the faithful after the presentation of a lighted candle.]

CELEBRATION OF CONFIRMATION

225 Between the celebration of baptism and confirmation, the congregation may sing a suitable song.

The place for the celebration of confirmation is either at the baptismal font or in the sanctuary, depending on the place where, according to local conditions, baptism has been celebrated.

226 If the bishop has conferred baptism, he should now also confer confirmation. If the bishop is not present, the priest who conferred baptism is authorized to confirm.

[When there are a great many persons to be confirmed, the minister of confirmation may associate priests with himself as ministers of the sacrament (see no. 14).]

INVITATION

227 The celebrant first speaks briefly to the newly baptised in these or similar words.

My dear newly baptised, born again in Christ by baptism, you have become members of Christ and of his priestly people. Now you are to share in the outpouring of the Holy Spirit among us, the Spirit sent by the Lord upon his apostles at Pentecost and given by them and their successors to the baptised.

The promised strength of the Holy Spirit, which you are to receive, will make you more like Christ and help you to be witnesses to his suffering, death, and resurrection. It will strengthen you to be active members of the Church and to build up the Body of Christ in faith and love.

[The priests who will be associated with the celebrant as ministers of the sacrament now stand next to him.]

With hands joined, the celebrant next addresses the people:

My dear friends, let us pray to God our Father, that he will pour out the Holy Spirit on these newly baptised to strengthen them with his gifts and anoint them to be more like Christ, the Son of God.

All pray briefly in silence.

LAYING ON OF HANDS

228 The celebrant holds his hands outstretched over the entire group of those to be confirmed and says the following prayer.

[In silence the priests associated as ministers of the sacrament also hold their hands outstretched over the candidates.]

All-powerful God, Father of our Lord Jesus Christ,
by water and the Holy Spirit
you freed your sons and daughters from sin
and gave them new life.

Send your Holy Spirit upon them
to be their helper and guide.

Give them the spirit of wisdom and understanding,
the spirit of right judgment and courage,
the spirit of knowledge and reverence.
Fill them with the spirit of wonder and awe in your presence.

We ask this through Christ our Lord.

R. Amen.

Anointing with Chrism

229 A minister brings the chrism to the celebrant. 231

[When the celebrant is the bishop, priests who are associated as ministers of the sacrament receive the chrism from him.]

Each candidate, with godparent or godparents, goes to the celebrant (or to an associated minister of the sacrament); or, if circumstances require, the celebrant (associated ministers) may go to the candidates.

Either or both godparents place the right hand on the shoulder of the candidate and either a godparent or the candidate gives the candidate's name to the minister of the sacrament. During the conferral of the sacrament a suitable song may be sung.

The minister of the sacrament dips his right thumb in the chrism and makes the sign of the cross on the forehead of the one to be confirmed as he says:

N., be sealed with the Gift of the Holy Spirit.

Newly confirmed:
Amen.

The minister of the sacrament adds:
Peace be with you.

Newly confirmed:
And also with you.

230 The renewal of baptismal promises by the congregation, as in the Roman Missal, 'Easter Vigil' (no. 46), follows the celebration of confirmation. Then the neophytes are led to their places among the faithful.

[Outside the Easter Vigil, the neophytes are led to their place among the faithful immediately after confirmation.]

LITURGY OF THE EUCHARIST

231 Since the profession of faith is not said, the general intercessions begin immediately and for the first time the neophytes take part in them. Some of the neophytes also take part in the procession to the altar with the gifts.

232 With Eucharistic Prayers I, II, or III the special interpolations given in the Roman Missal, the ritual Masses, 'Christian Initiation: Baptism' are used.

[Eucharistic Prayer IV, with its special interpolation indicated in the same ritual Masses, may also be used but outside the Easter Vigil.]

233 It is most desirable that the neophytes, together with their godparents, parents, spouses, and catechists, receive communion under both kinds.

Before saying 'This is the Lamb of God,' the celebrant may briefly remind the neophytes of the preeminence of the eucharist, which is the climax of their initiation and the centre of the whole Christian life.

PERIOD OF POSTBAPTISMAL CATECHESIS OR MYSTAGOGY

*You are a chosen race, a royal priesthood, a holy people; praise God
who called you out of darkness and into his marvellous light*

234 The third step of Christian initiation, the celebration of the sacra- 37
ments, is followed by the final period, the period of postbaptismal catechesis or mystagogy. This is a time for the community and the neophytes
together to grow in deepening their grasp of the paschal mystery and in
making it part of their lives through meditation on the Gospel, sharing
in the eucharist, and doing the works of charity. To strengthen the neo- *Newly*
phytes as they begin to walk in newness of life, the community of the faith- *Baptised*
ful, their godparents, and their parish priests (pastors) should give them
thoughtful and friendly help.

235 The neophytes are, as the term 'mystagogy' suggests, introduced into 38
a fuller and more effective understanding of mysteries through the Gospel
message they have learned and above all through their experience of the
sacraments they have received. For they have truly been renewed in mind,
tasted more deeply the sweetness of God's word, received the fellowship
of the Holy Spirit, and grown to know the goodness of the Lord. Out of
this experience, which belongs to Christians and increases as it is lived,
they derive a new perception of the faith, of the Church, and of the world.

236 Just as their new participation in the sacraments enlightens the neo- 39
phytes' understanding of the Scriptures, so too it increases their contact 235
with the rest of the faithful and has an impact on the experience of the
community. As a result, interaction between the neophytes and the faithful is made easier and more beneficial. The period of postbaptismal catechesis is of great significance for both the neophytes and the rest of the faithful.
Through it the neophytes, with the help of their godparents, should experience a full and joyful welcome into the community and enter into closer
ties with the other faithful. The faithful, in turn, should derive from it a
renewal of inspiration and of outlook.

237 Since the distinctive spirit and power of the period of postbaptismal 40
catechesis or mystagogy derive from the new, personal experience of the
sacraments and of the community, its main setting is the so-called Masses
for neophytes, that is, the Sunday Masses of the Easter season. Besides
being occasions for the newly baptised to gather with the community and
share in the mysteries, these celebrations include particularly suitable readings from the Lectionary, especially the readings for Year A. Even when
Christian initiation has been celebrated outside the usual times, the texts
for these Sunday Masses of the Easter season may be used.

238 All the neophytes and their godparents should make an effort to take part in the Masses for the neophytes and the entire local community should be invited to participate with them. Special places in the congregation are to be reserved for the neophytes and their godparents. The homily and, as circumstances suggest, the general intercessions should take into account the presence and needs of the neophytes.

239 To close the period of postbaptismal catechesis, some sort of celebra- tion should be held at the end of the Easter season near Pentecost Sunday; festivities in keeping with local custom may accompany the occasion.

240 On the anniversary of their baptism the neophytes should be brought together in order to give thanks to God, to share with one another their spiritual experiences, and to renew their commitment.

241 To show his pastoral concern for these new members of the Church, the bishop, particularly if he was unable to preside at the sacraments of initiation himself, should arrange, if possible, to meet the recently baptised at least once in the year and to preside at a celebration of the eucharist with them. At this Mass they may receive holy communion under both kinds.

Part II
RITES FOR PARTICULAR CIRCUMSTANCES

God loved the world so much, he gave us his only Son,
that all who believe in him might have eternal life

1 CHRISTIAN INITIATION OF CHILDREN WHO HAVE REACHED CATECHETICAL AGE

Do not keep the children from me

242 This form of the rite of Christian initiation is intended for children, not baptised as infants, who have attained the use of reason and are of catechetical age. They seek Christian initiation either at the direction of their parents or guardians or, with parental permission, on their own initiative. Such children are capable of receiving and nurturing a personal faith and of recognizing an obligation in conscience. But they cannot yet be treated as adults because, at this stage of their lives, they are dependent on their parents or guardians and are still strongly influenced by their companions and their social surroundings.

243 The Christian initiation of these children requires both a conversion that is personal and somewhat developed, in proportion to their age, and the assistance of the education they need. The process of initiation thus must be adapted both to their spiritual progress, that is, to the children's growth in faith, and to the catechetical instruction they receive. Accordingly, as with adults, their initiation is to be extended over several years, if need be, before they receive the sacraments. Also as with adults, their initiation is marked by several steps, the liturgical rites of acceptance into the order of catechumens (nos. 250-266), penitential rites or scrutinies (nos. 267-279), and the celebration of the sacraments of initiation (nos. 280-305); corresponding to the periods of adult initiation are the periods of the children's catechetical formation that lead up to and follow the steps of their initiation.

244 The children's progress in the formation they receive depends on the help and example of their companions and on the influence of their parents. Both these factors should therefore be taken into account.

1. Since the children to be initiated often belong to a group of children of the same age who are already baptised and are preparing for confirmation and eucharist, their initiation progresses gradually and within the supportive setting of this group of companions.

2. It is to be hoped that the children will also receive as much help and example as possible from the parents, whose permission is required for the children to be initiated and to live the Christian life. The period of initiation will also provide a good opportunity for the family to have contact with priests and catechists.

245 For the celebrations proper to this form of Christian initiation, it is advantageous, as circumstances allow, to form a group of several children who are in this same situation, in order that by example they may help one another in their progress as catechumens.

246 In regard to the time for the celebration of the steps of initiation, it is preferable that, if possible, the final period of preparation, begun by the second step, the penitential rites, coincide with Lent and that the final step, celebration of the sacraments of initiation, take place at the Easter Vigil (see no. 8). Nevertheless before the children are admitted to the sacraments at Easter, it should be established that they are ready for the sacraments. Celebration at this time must also be consistent with the programme of catechetical instruction they are receiving, since the candidates should, if possible, come to the sacraments of initiation at the time that their baptised companions are to receive confirmation or eucharist.

247 For children of this age, at the rites during the process of initiation, it is generally preferable not to have the whole parish community present, but simply represented. Thus these rites should be celebrated with the active participation of a congregation that consists of a suitable number of the faithful, the parents, family, members of the catechetical group, and a few adult friends.

248 Each conference of bishops may adapt and add to the form of the rite given here, in order that the rite will more effectively satisfy local needs, conditions, and pastoral requirements. The rites for the presentation of the Creed (nos. 144-149) and the Lord's Prayer (nos. 165-170), adapted to the age of the children, may be incorporated. When the form of the rite of initiation for children is translated, the instructions and prayers should be adapted to their understanding. Furthermore, in addition to any liturgical text translated from the Latin *editio typica*, the conference of bishops may also approve an original, alternative text that says the same thing in a way more suited to children (see *Christian Initiation*, General Introduction, no. 32).

249 In following this form of the rite of Christian initiation the celebrant should make full and wise use of the options mentioned in *Christian Initiation*, General Introduction (nos. 34-35), in the *Rite of Baptism for Children*, Introduction (no. 31), and in the *Rite of Christian Initiation of Adults*, Introduction (no. 35).

FIRST STEP: ACCEPTANCE INTO THE ORDER OF CATECHUMENS

Happy the people the Lord has chosen to be his own

250 It is important that this rite be celebrated with an actively participating but small congregation, since the presence of a large group might make the children uncomfortable (see no. 247). When possible, the children's parents or guardians should be present. If they cannot come, they should indicate that they have given consent to their children and their place should be taken by 'sponsors' (see no. 10), that is, suitable members of the Church who act on this occasion for the parents and present the children. The presiding celebrant is a priest or deacon. 314

251 The celebration takes place in the church or in a place that, according to the age and understanding of the children, can help them to experience a warm welcome. As circumstances suggest, the first part of the rite, 'Receiving the Children,' is carried out at the entrance of the place chosen for the celebration, and the second part of the rite, 'Liturgy of the Word,' takes place inside. 315
329

The celebration is not normally combined with celebration of the eucharist.

OUTLINE OF THE RITE

RECEIVING THE CHILDREN

Greeting
Opening Dialogue
Affirmation by the Parents (Sponsors)
  and the Assembly
Signing of the Candidates with the Cross
    Signing of the Forehead
    [Signing of the Other Senses]
Invitation to the Celebration of the Word of God

LITURGY OF THE WORD

Instruction
Readings
Homily
[Presentation of a Bible]
Intercessions for the Children
Prayer over the Children
Dismissal

RITE OF ACCEPTANCE INTO THE ORDER OF CATECHUMENS

RECEIVING THE CHILDREN

252 The priest or deacon, wearing an alb or surplice with stole, comes to the place where the children are waiting with their parents or guardians or, alternatively, with their sponsors. 316

GREETING

253 The celebrant and the community present greet the children simply and in a friendly manner. The celebrant then speaks to the children and their parents or sponsors, pointing out the joy and happiness of the Church at their presence. Next he invites the children and their parents or sponsors to come forward and stand before him. 316
317

OPENING DIALOGUE

254 The celebrant then asks the children individually to express their intention. He may do so by means of such questions and answers as those given here or he may use other words that will allow the children to give such answers as: 'I want to do the will of God'; 'I want to follow the word of God'; 'I want to be baptised'; 'I want to be a friend of Jesus Christ'; 'I want to join the Christian family.' 318

[If there are a great many children, the celebrant may question a few of them and then ask the rest to express agreement with the responses given.]

Celebrant:

What do you want to become?

Children:

A Christian.

Celebrant:

Why do you want to become a Christian?

Children:

Because I believe in Christ.

Celebrant:

What do you gain by believing in Christ?

Children:

Eternal life.

The celebrant concludes this opening dialogue with a brief catechesis, suited to the children's age and circumstances, on the step they are taking. He may use these or similar words and may ask the children, as a sign of their assent, to repeat the final quotation from the words of Christ.

Since you already believe in Christ and want us to prepare you for baptism, we welcome you joyfully into our Christian family, where you will come to know Christ better day by day. Together with us you will try to live as children of God, for our Lord has taught us: 'Love God with all your heart and love one another as I have loved you.'

Affirmation by the Parents (Sponsors) and the Assembly

255 In the following or a similar way, the celebrant asks the children to seek the consent of the parents or sponsors who are presenting them.

N. and N., go and ask your parents (sponsors) to come here and stand with you so that they may give their assent.

The children go to their parents or sponsors and bring them before the celebrant, who continues:

Dear parents (sponsors), your children have asked to be prepared for baptism. Do you consent to their request?

Parents or sponsors:

We do.

Celebrant:

Are you willing to do your part in their preparation for baptism?

Parents or sponsors:

We are.

Then the celebrant questions the assembly, using these or similar words.

These boys and girls have set out on the road to baptism. They will need the support of our faith and love. Are you, their families and friends, ready to give that help?

All:
We are.

SIGNING OF THE CANDIDATES WITH THE CROSS

256 Next the cross is traced on the forehead of each child (or in front of the forehead, if the conference of bishops deems this more suitable); at the discretion of the celebrant, and especially if the children are somewhat older, the signing of the other senses may follow. The celebrant alone says the formularies accompanying each signing.

SIGNING OF THE FOREHEAD

257 The celebrant first says the following formulary.

N. and N. Christ has called you to be his friends. Always remember him and be faithful to him.

Therefore I mark your forehead with the sign of the cross. It is the sign of Christians; let it remind you always of Christ and how much he loves you.

Then the celebrant goes to the children and in silence traces the cross on the forehead of each one.

Then, if there is to be no signing of the other senses, he may, in the following words, invite the parents or sponsors and the catechists to trace the sign of the cross on their candidate's forehead.

And I also invite you, parents (sponsors) and catechists [N. and N.], since you also belong to Christ, to sign the children with the sign of the cross.

All sing or say the following or another suitable acclamation.
Glory and praise to you, Lord Jesus Christ!

258 The signing of the other senses may be carried out by the celebrant, who says the following formulary for each child. The signing of the candidates may also be carried out by their parents or sponsors or by their catechists, as the celebrant says the formulary in the plural over all the children at once. After the signing of each sense the assembly may sing or recite an acclamation in praise of Christ, for example, 'Glory and praise to you, Lord Jesus Christ!'

While the ears are being signed the celebrant says:

I [we] mark your ears with the sign of the cross: hear the words of Christ.

While the eyes are being signed:

I [we] mark your eyes with the sign of the cross: see the works of Christ.

While the lips are being signed:

I [we] mark your lips with the sign of the cross: speak as Christ would speak.

While the breast is being signed:

I [we] mark the sign of the cross over your heart: make your heart the home of Christ.

While the shoulders are being signed:

I [we] mark your shoulders with the sign of the cross: be strong with the strength of Christ.

While the sign of the cross is traced above the whole person:

I [we] place you entirely under the sign of Christ's cross in the name of the Father, and of the Son, ✠ and of the Holy Spirit: live with Jesus now and for ever.

Child:

Amen.

INVITATION TO THE CELEBRATION OF THE WORD OF GOD

259 After the signing, the celebrant in the following or similar words invites the children and their parents or sponsors to enter the church or other place chosen for the celebration. Once the invitation has been spoken, the children enter and take places either with their parents or sponsors or with the baptised companions of their catechetical group (see no. 244,1), so that it is clear that they now are a part of the assembly. During the entrance, Psalm 94(95) or Psalm 121(122) is sung or another suitable song.

Celebrant:

Now you can take your place in the Christian assembly. Come with us to listen to the Lord as he speaks and to join us in prayer.

LITURGY OF THE WORD

INSTRUCTION

260 When the children have reached their places, the celebrant speaks to them briefly, helping them to understand the dignity of God's word, which is proclaimed and heard in the Christian assembly.

325

The Lectionary or the Bible is carried in procession and placed with honour on the lectern, where it may be incensed.

Celebration of the liturgy of the word follows.

READINGS

Scripture readings are chosen that can be adapted to the understanding of the children and to their progress in the catechetical formation they and their companions have received. Such readings may be chosen from those given in the Lectionary for Mass, ritual Masses, 'Christian Initiation apart from the Easter Vigil' or from elsewhere in the Lectionary; the following texts (Lectionary, Vol. III, pp. 48-50; other readings, Vol. III, pp. 50-55) may also be used.

326

FIRST READING
Genesis 12:1-4a—*Abraham is called by God.*

Psalm 32(:33):4-5, 12-13, 18-19, 20 and 22
R. (v.12b) **Happy the people the Lord has chosen as his own.**
Or:
R. (v.22) **May your love be upon us, O Lord,**
as we place all our trust in you.

VERSE BEFORE THE GOSPEL

John 1:41, 17b
We have found the Messiah — which means the Christ —
grace and truth have come through him.

GOSPEL

John 1:35-42 — *Look, there is the lamb of God. We have found the Messiah.*

HOMILY

262 The celebrant then gives a brief homily in explanation of   32
the readings.

It is recommended that after the homily he invite the children
to spend a period in silent prayer.

Then a suitable song is sung.

PRESENTATION OF A BIBLE

263 During or after the song, a book containing the Gospels   32
may be presented to the children. They should be prepared for
this presentation either beforehand in the homily or by a few
words of explanation at this moment.

INTERCESSIONS FOR THE CHILDREN

264 The intercessions follow in these or similar words.   329

Celebrant:
Let us pray for these children, your sons and daughters, your
companions and friends, as they draw nearer to God.

Assisting minister:

That they may steadily increase their desire to live with Jesus, let us pray to the Lord:

R. Lord, hear our prayer.

Assisting minister:

That by belonging to the Church they may find true happiness, let us pray to the Lord:

R. Lord, hear our prayer.

Assisting minister:

That they may be given the strength to persevere in their preparation for baptism, let us pray to the Lord:

R. Lord, hear our prayer.

Assisting minister:

That they may be preserved from the temptation of discouragement and fear, let us pray to the Lord:

R. Lord, hear our prayer.

Assisting minister:

That they may rejoice in the happiness of receiving the sacraments of baptism, confirmation, and the eucharist, let us pray to the Lord:

R. Lord, hear our prayer.

PRAYER OVER THE CHILDREN

265 After the intercessions, the celebrant, with hands outstretched over the children, says the following prayer. 329

Lord,
you have filled these children
with the desire to become perfect Christians.
As they grow in wisdom and knowledge,
respond to their hopes
and answer our prayers.

We ask this through Christ our Lord.

R. Amen.

DISMISSAL

266 After the prayer the children and the community are dismissed and a suitable song concludes the celebration. But if for some reason the eucharist is to be celebrated (see no. 251), the children are dismissed beforehand.

Celebrant:

**Go in peace,
and may the Lord remain with you always.**

All:

Thanks be to God.

SECOND STEP: PENITENTIAL RITES (SCRUTINIES)

Create in me a new heart and a new spirit

267 These penitential rites, which mark the second step in the children's Christian initiation, are major occasions in their catechumenate. They are held within a celebration of the word of God as a kind of scrutiny, similar to the scrutinies in the adult rite. Thus the guidelines given for the adult rite (nos. 128-133) may be followed and adapted, since the children's penitential rites have a similar purpose.   330

268 Because the penitential rites normally belong to the period of final preparation for baptism, the condition for their celebration is that the children are approaching the maturity of faith and understanding requisite for baptism.   331

269 Along with the children, their godparents and their baptised companions from the catechetical group participate in the celebration of these penitential rites. Therefore the rites are to be adapted in such a way that they also benefit the participants who are not catechumens. In particular, these penitential rites are a proper occasion for baptised children of the catechetical group to celebrate the sacrament of penance for the first time. When this is the case, care should be taken to include explanations, prayers, and ritual acts that relate to the celebration of the sacrament with these children.   332

270 The penitential rites are celebrated during Lent, if the catechumens are to be initiated at Easter; if not, at the most suitable time. At least one penitential rite is to be celebrated, and, if this can be arranged conveniently, a second should follow after an appropriate interval. The texts for a second celebration are to be composed on the model of the first given here, but the texts for the intercessions and prayer of exorcism given in the adult rite (nos. 140-141, 154-155, 161-162) are used, with the requisite modifications.   333

OUTLINE OF THE RITE

LITURGY OF THE WORD

Greeting and Introduction
Prayer
Readings
Homily
Intercessions
Exorcism
Anointing with the Oil of Catechumens
or Laying on of Hands
Dismissal of the Children

LITURGY OF PENANCE

PENITENTIAL RITE (SCRUTINY)

LITURGY OF THE WORD

Greeting and Introduction

271 The priest welcomes the assembly and in a few words explains that the rite will have different meanings for the different participants: the children who are catechumens, the children who are already baptised, particularly those who will celebrate the sacrament of penance for the first time, the parents, godparents, catechists, priests, etc. All these participants in their own different ways are going to hear the comforting message of pardon for sin, for which they will praise the Father's mercy. 334

A song may be sung that joyfully expresses faith in the mercy of God our Father.

Prayer

272 The celebrant then says one of the following prayers. 335

A   God of pardon and mercy,
you reveal yourself in your readiness to forgive
and manifest your glory by making us holy.

Grant that we who repent
may be cleansed from sin
and restored to your life of grace.

We ask this through Christ our Lord.

R. Amen.

B   Lord,
grant us your pardon and peace,
so that, cleansed of our sins,
we may serve you with untroubled hearts.

We ask this through Christ our Lord.

R. Amen.

READINGS

273 One or several readings may be chosen from those in the following list (Lectionary, Vol. III, pp. 55-58); if there is more than one reading, one of the responsorial psalms listed here from the ritual Masses, 'Christian Initiation apart from the Easter Vigil' (or any of the others from the same Mass) or a song should be used between the readings.

READINGS

1   Ezekiel 36:25-28 — *A new heart and a new spirit.*
2   Isaiah 1:16-18 — *The cleansing of sinners.*
3   1 John 1:8 — 2:2 — *Jesus Christ is our saviour.*
4   Mark 1:1-5, 14-15 — *Repent and believe the Good News.*
5   Mark 2:1-12 — *The story of the paralytic.*
6   Luke 15:1-7 — *The sheep that was lost and then found.*

Or the gospels used in the scrutinies of the adult rite:

7   John 4:5-15, 19-26, 39-42 (Vol. I, pp. 249-250)
    — *A spring of water welling up to eternal life.*
8   John 9:1, 6-9, 13-17, 34-39 (Vol. I, p. 280)
    — *He went off and washed himself, and came away with his sight restored.*
9   John 11:3-7, 17, 20-27, 33b-45 (Vol. I, pp. 308-309)
    — *I am the resurrection and the life.*

RESPONSORIAL PSALMS

If more than one reading is used, psalms or songs should be sung between the readings, chosen from those given for the initiation of adults, (Vol. III, pp. 18ff).

1   Psalm 22(23):1-3a, 3b-4, 5-6 (Vol. III, p. 20)
    R. (v.1) **The Lord is my shepherd;
    there is nothing I shall want.**
2   Psalm 26(27):1, 4, 8b-9abc, 13-14 (Vol. III, p. 31)
    R. (v.1a) **The Lord is my light and my help.**
3   Psalm 31(32):1-2, 5, 11 (Vol. III, p. 27)
    R. (v.1a) **Happy the man whose offence is forgiven.**
4   Psalm 88(89):3-4, 16-17, 21-22, 25, 27 (Vol. III, p. 19)
    R. (v.2a) **I will sing for ever of your love, O Lord.**

HOMILY

274 After the readings the celebrant explains the sacred texts in a short homily.

During the homily or immediately after it, the celebrant prepares all those in the assembly for conversion and repentance by speaking to them of appropriate themes, then pausing for periods of silent reflection.

If the assembly includes baptised children who will receive the sacrament of penance for the first time, the celebrant turns to them and invites them to show by some external sign their faith in Christ the Saviour and their sorrow for their sins.

275 After a brief interval of silence to lead all present to sincere sorrow for sin, the celebrant introduces the following intercessions with an invitation addressed to the assembly.

For the celebrant's introduction and the intentions of the intercessions the texts in the adult rite (nos. 140, 154, and 161) may also be used, with the requisite modifications.

Celebrant:

Let us pray for N. and N., who are preparing themselves for the sacraments of Christian initiation, [for N. and N., who will receive God's forgiveness in the sacrament of penance for the first time,] and for ourselves, who seek the mercy of Christ.

Assisting minister:

That we may open our hearts to the Lord Jesus with gratitude and faith, let us pray to the Lord:

R. Lord, hear our prayer.

Assisting minister:

That we may honestly try to know our failures and recognise our sins, let us pray to the Lord:

R. Lord, hear our prayer.

Assisting minister:

That, as children of God, we may openly admit our weaknesses and faults, let us pray to the Lord:

R. Lord, hear our prayer.

Assisting minister:

That in the presence of Christ we may express sorrow for our sins, let us pray to the Lord:

R. Lord, hear our prayer.

Assisting minister:

That we may be delivered from present evils and protected against those to come, let us pray to the Lord:

R. Lord, hear our prayer.

Assisting minister:

That we may learn from our Father in heaven to triumph by his love over the powers of sin, let us pray to the Lord:

R. Lord, hear our prayer.

276 Then the celebrant, with hands outstretched over the children, says one of the following.

Let us pray.

A   **Father of mercies,**
you sent your only Son
to rescue us from the slavery of sin
and to give us freedom as your children.

Look with love on these young people and fulfil their hopes;
they have already experienced temptation
and they acknowledge their faults.

Lead them from darkness into your unfailing light,
cleanse them from sin,
let them know the joy of your peace,
and guide them safely through life.

We ask this through Christ our Lord.

R. **Amen.**

B   **God of mercy and Father of all,**
look upon N. and N., who will soon be baptised.

Children:
We have heard the words of Jesus
and we love them.

Celebrant:
Even though they try to live as your children,
they sometimes find this difficult.

Children:
Father, we want always to do what pleases you,
but sometimes we find this hard.

Celebrant:
Loving Father,
free these young people
from whatever could make them bad
and help them always to walk in your light.

Children:

**We want to walk with Jesus,
who gave his life for us.
Help us, Father, to follow him.**

Celebrant:

**If they stumble on the way
and do not please you,
help them up with the power of your hand,
that they may rise again
and continue on their journey to you
with Jesus Christ our Lord.**

Children:

Father, give us strength.

Anointing with the Oil of Catechumens or Laying on of Hands

277 The rite continues with the anointing with the oil of catechumens, option A. But if by decision of the conference of bishops this anointing is to be omitted altogether (see no. 33,7) or if it is to be deferred until the celebration of baptism (no. 291), the present rite continues with a laying on of hands, option B.

340

A   Anointing with the Oil of Catechumens: The celebrant faces the children and says:

**We anoint you with the oil of salvation
in the name of Christ our Saviour.
May he strengthen you with his power,
who lives and reigns for ever and ever.**

Children:

Amen.

Each child is anointed with the oil of catechumens on the breast or on both hands or even on other parts of the body, if this seems desirable.

B LAYING ON OF HANDS: The celebrant faces the children and says:

**May Christ our Saviour
strengthen you with his power,
for he is Lord for ever and ever.**

Children:

Amen.

> Then, in silence, the celebrant lays his hands on the head of each child.

DISMISSAL OF THE CHILDREN

278 The celebrant dismisses the children, option A, or else sends them back to their places in the church, where they remain, option B.

A The celebrant dismisses the children, using these or similar words.

N. and N., here among us the Lord Jesus has opened the arms of his mercy to you. Go now in peace.

Children:

Thanks be to God.

B The celebrant sends the children back to their places in the church, using these or similar words.

N. and N., here among us the Lord Jesus has opened the arms of his mercy to you. Return to your places now and continue with us in prayer.

Children:

Thanks be to God.

LITURGY OF PENANCE

279 Next, the liturgy of the sacrament of penance begins for baptised children who will celebrate this sacrament for the first time. After the celebrant gives a brief instruction, individual confession, first of the children, then of the others in the assembly, follows.

A suitable song or a prayer of thanksgiving follows the celebration of the sacrament; all then leave.

THIRD STEP: CELEBRATION OF THE SACRAMENTS OF INITIATION

Wake up and rise from death: Christ will shine upon you

280 In order to bring out the paschal character of baptism, celebration   343
of the sacraments of initiation should preferably take place at the Easter
Vigil or on a Sunday, the day that the Church devotes to the remembrance
of Christ's resurrection (see *Rite of Baptism for Children*, Introduction, no.
9). But the provisions of no. 246 should also guide the choice of time for
the celebration of the sacraments of initiation.

281 At this third step of their Christian initiation, the children will re-   344
ceive the sacrament of baptism, the bishop or priest who baptises them
will also confer confirmation, and the children will for the first time participate in the liturgy of the eucharist.

282 If the sacraments of initiation are celebrated at a time other than the   345
Easter Vigil or Easter Sunday, the Mass of the day or one of the ritual
Masses in the Roman Missal, 'Christian Initiation: Baptism' is used. The
readings are chosen from those given in the Lectionary for Mass, 'Celebration of the Sacraments of Initiation apart from the Easter Vigil' (Vol.
III, pp. 18-47); but the readings for the Sunday or feast on which the celebration takes place may be used instead.

283 All the children to be baptised are to be accompanied by their own   346
godparent or godparents, chosen by themselves and approved by the priest
(see no. 11; *Christian Initiation*, General Introduction, no. 10).

284 Baptised children of the catechetical group may be completing their
Christian initiation in the sacraments of confirmation and the eucharist
at this same celebration. When the bishop himself will not be the celebrant,
he should grant the faculty to confirm such children to the priest who will
be the celebrant.[1] For their confirmation, previously baptised children of
the catechetical group are to have their own sponsors. If possible, these
should be the persons who were godparents for their baptism, but other
qualified persons may be chosen.[2]

---

[1] See *Rite of Confirmation*, Introduction, no. 7, b.

[2] See ibid., nos. 5 and 6.

OUTLINE OF THE RITE

LITURGY OF THE WORD

CELEBRATION OF BAPTISM

Invitation to Prayer
Prayer over the Water
[Community's Profession of Faith]
Children's Profession of Faith
    Renunciation of Sin
    [Anointing with the Oil of Catechumens]
    Profession of Faith
Baptism
Explanatory Rites
    [Anointing after Baptism]
    [Clothing with a Baptismal Garment]
    Presentation of a Lighted Candle

CELEBRATION OF CONFIRMATION

Invitation
Laying on of Hands
Anointing with Chrism

LITURGY OF THE EUCHARIST

CELEBRATION OF THE SACRAMENTS OF INITIATION

LITURGY OF THE WORD

285 When the children who are candidates for initiation, their parents or guardians, godparents, other children from the catechetical group, friends, and members of the parish have assembled, Mass begins.

347

The texts for the Mass and the readings in the liturgy of the word are those already indicated in no. 282 (Lectionary for Mass, Vol. III, pp. 18-47; the readings for the Sunday or feast on which the celebration takes place may be used instead). The homily follows the readings.

CELEBRATION OF BAPTISM

Invitation to Prayer

286 After the homily, the celebrant and the children with their parents or guardians and godparents go to the baptismal font, if this is in view of the faithful; otherwise they gather in the sanctuary, where a vessel of water should be prepared beforehand. The celebrant speaks to the family, friends, and the entire assembly in these or similar words.

348

Dear friends, N. and N., with the approval of their parents, have asked to be baptised. Let us call upon the Father to number them among his adopted children in Christ.

Prayer over the Water

287 Next, the celebrant blesses the water or says a prayer of thanksgiving over the water.

349
350

When baptism is celebrated at the Easter Vigil, the celebrant blesses the water, using option A; outside the Easter Vigil, in blessing the water he may use either option A or the other blessing formularies given in no. 215 as options B and C.

But when baptism is celebrated during the Easter season and water already blessed at the Easter Vigil is available, the celebrant uses option B, so that this part of the celebration will retain the themes of thanksgiving and intercession; he may also use the second Easter-season thanksgiving formulary given in no. 215 as option E.

A   BLESSING OF THE WATER: Facing the font (or vessel) containing the water, the celebrant says the following (music, p. 126):

Father,
you give us grace through sacramental signs,
which tell us of the wonders of your unseen power.

In baptism we use your gift of water,
which you have made a rich symbol of the grace
you give us in this sacrament.

At the very dawn of creation
your Spirit breathed on the waters,
making them the wellspring of all holiness.

The waters of the great flood
you made a sign of the waters of baptism
that make an end of sin
and a new beginning of goodness.

Through the waters of the Red Sea
you led Israel out of slavery
to be an image of God's holy people,
set free from sin by baptism.

In the waters of the Jordan
your Son was baptised by John
and anointed with the Spirit.

Your Son willed that water and blood should flow from his side
as he hung upon the cross.

After his resurrection he told his disciples:
'Go out and teach all nations,
baptising them in the name of the Father, and of the Son,
    and of the Holy Spirit.'

Father,
look now with love upon your Church
and unseal for it the fountain of baptism.

By the power of the Holy Spirit
give to this water the grace of your Son,
so that in the sacrament of baptism
all those whom you have created in your likeness
may be cleansed from sin
and rise to a new birth of innocence
by water and the Holy Spirit.

> The celebrant before continuing touches the water with his right
> hand.

> [But at the Easter Vigil, if this can be done conveniently, the
> celebrant before continuing lowers the Easter candle into the wa-
> ter once or three times, then holds it there until the acclamation
> at the end of the blessing.]

We ask you, Father, with your Son
to send the Holy Spirit upon the waters of this font.
May all who are buried with Christ in the death of baptism
rise also with him to newness of life.
We ask this through Christ our Lord.

> All:

Amen.

> The people sing the following or some other suitable acclamation.

Springs of water, bless the Lord.
Give him glory and praise for ever.

B   EASTER-SEASON THANKSGIVING OVER WATER ALREADY BLESSED: 389
> Facing the font (or vessel) containing the blessed water, the cel-
> ebrant says the following.

Praise to you, almighty God and Father,
for you have created water to cleanse and to give life.

> All sing or say the following or some other suitable acclamation.

Blessed be God.

> Celebrant:

Praise to you, Lord Jesus Christ, the Father's only Son,
for you offered yourself on the cross,
that in the blood and water flowing from your side
and through your death and resurrection
the Church might be born.

All:

Blessed be God.

Celebrant:

Praise to you, God the Holy Spirit,
for you anointed Christ at his baptism in the waters
of the Jordan,
that we might all be baptised in you.

All:

Blessed be God.

The celebrant concludes with the following prayer.

You have called your children, N. and N., to this cleansing water,
that they may share in the faith of your Church
and have eternal life.
By the mystery of this consecrated water
lead them to a new and spiritual birth.

We ask this through Christ our Lord.

All:

Amen.

COMMUNITY'S PROFESSION OF FAITH

288 Before the rite of the children's profession of faith, the celebrant may, if this is in keeping with the circumstances, invite the parents or guardians, godparents, and all present to profess their faith.

N. and N. have completed a long preparation and are ready for baptism. They will receive new life from God who is love: they will become Christians.

From now on, we will need to help them even more. This is especially true of you, their parents, who have given them permission to be baptised and who have the primary responsibility for their upbringing. But all of us who have in any way prepared them to meet Christ today must always be ready to assist them.

And so, before these children make their profession of faith in our presence, let us in their presence publicly and with a deep sense of responsibility renew our own profession of faith, which is the faith of the Church.

> Then together with the celebrant all recite the profession of faith, using either the Apostles' Creed, option A, or the Nicene Creed, option B.

A APOSTLES' CREED

> All join the celebrant and say:

I believe in God, the Father almighty,
  creator of heaven and earth.

I believe in Jesus Christ, his only Son, our Lord.
  He was conceived by the power of the Holy Spirit
    and born of the Virgin Mary.
  He suffered under Pontius Pilate,
    was crucified, died, and was buried.
  He descended to the dead.
  On the third day he rose again.
  He ascended into heaven,
    and is seated at the right hand of the Father.
  He will come again to judge the living and the dead.

I believe in the Holy Spirit,
  the holy catholic Church,
  the communion of saints,
  the forgiveness of sins,
  the resurrection of the body,
  and the life everlasting. Amen.

B NICENE CREED

> All join the celebrant and say:

We believe in one God,
  the Father, the Almighty,
  maker of heaven and earth,
  of all that is, seen and unseen.

We believe in one Lord, Jesus Christ,
the only Son of God,
eternally begotten of the Father,
God from God, Light from Light,
true God from true God,
begotten, not made,
of one Being with the Father.
Through him all things were made.
For us men and for our salvation
he came down from heaven:
by the power of the Holy Spirit
he became incarnate from the Virgin Mary,
and was made man.
For our sake he was crucified under Pontius Pilate;
he suffered death and was buried.
On the third day he rose again
in accordance with the Scriptures;
he ascended into heaven
and is seated at the right hand of the Father.
He will come again in glory to judge the living and the dead,
and his kingdom will have no end.

We believe in the Holy Spirit, the Lord, the giver of life,
who proceeds from the Father and the Son.
With the Father and the Son he is worshipped and glorified.
He has spoken through the Prophets.
We believe in one holy catholic and apostolic Church.
We acknowledge one baptism for the forgiveness of sins.
We look for the resurrection of the dead,
and the life of the world to come. Amen.

CHILDREN'S PROFESSION OF FAITH

289 The celebration of baptism continues with the rite of the
children's renunciation of sin and profession of faith.

The celebrant first addresses them briefly in these or similar
words.

Children [N. and N.], you have spent a long time in preparation and you have now asked to be baptised. Your parents have

agreed to your request; your teachers, companions, and friends have helped you; and all who have come here today promise you the example of their faith and their loving support.

Before you are baptised, reject Satan and profess your faith here in the presence of God's Church.

RENUNCIATION OF SIN

290 The celebrant, using one of the following formularies, questions all the children together.

A

Celebrant:
Do you reject sin so as to live in the freedom of God's children?

Children:
I do.

Celebrant:
**Do you reject the glamour of evil,
and refuse to be mastered by sin?**

Children:
I do.

Celebrant:
Do you reject Satan, father of sin and prince of darkness?

Children:
I do.

B

Celebrant:
**Do you reject Satan,
and all his works,
and all his empty promises?**

Children:
I do.

Anointing with the Oil of Catechumens

291 Unless the conference of bishops has decided on its omission (see no. 33,7), or it has already been celebrated during the penitential rite (no. 277), the anointing with the oil of catechumens takes place between the renunciation and the profession of faith.

The celebrant, facing the children, says:

**We anoint you with the oil of salvation
in the name of Christ our Saviour.
May he strengthen you with his power,
who lives and reigns for ever and ever.**

Children:

Amen.

Each of the children is anointed with the oil of catechumens on both hands, on the breast, or on other parts of the body, if this seems desirable.

[If there are a great number of children, additional priests or deacons may assist with the anointings.]

Profession of Faith

292 The celebrant, informed by the godparents of the name of each child, asks the child individually to make the profession of faith, then immediately baptises the child.

Celebrant:

**N., do you believe in God, the Father almighty,
creator of heaven and earth?**

Child:

I do.

Celebrant:

**Do you believe in Jesus Christ, his only Son, our Lord,
who was born of the Virgin Mary,
was crucified, died, and was buried,
rose from the dead,
and is now seated at the right hand of the Father?**

Child:

I do.

Celebrant:

Do you believe in the Holy Spirit,
the holy catholic Church, the communion of saints,
the forgiveness of sins, the resurrection of the body,
and the life everlasting?

Child:

I do.

BAPTISM

293 The celebrant baptises each child either by immersion, option A, or by the pouring of water, option B. Each baptism may be followed by a short acclamation (Appendix, no. 452), sung or said by the people.

[If there are a great number of children to be baptised, they may be divided into groups and baptised by assisting priests or deacons. In baptising, either by immersion, option A, or by the pouring of water, option B, these ministers say the sacramental formulary for each child. During the baptisms, singing by the people is desirable or readings from Scripture or simply silent prayer.]

356

A

If baptism is by immersion, of the whole body or of the head only, decency and decorum should be preserved. Either or both godparents touch the child. The celebrant, immersing the child's whole body or head three times, baptises the child in the name of the Trinity.

220

N., I baptise you in the name of the Father,

He immerses the child the first time.

and of the Son,

He immerses the child the second time.

and of the Holy Spirit.

He immerses the child the third time.

B If baptism is by the pouring of water, either or both godparents
place the right hand on the shoulder of the child, and the celebrant, taking baptismal water and pouring it three times on the
child's bowed head, baptises the child in the name of the Trinity.

N., I baptise you in the name of the Father,

He pours water the first time.

and of the Son,

He pours water the second time.

and of the Holy Spirit.

He pours water the third time.

EXPLANATORY RITES

294 The celebration of baptism proceeds immediately with the
explanatory rites, after which the celebration of confirmation normally follows. 3

ANOINTING AFTER BAPTISM

295 If the confirmation of those baptised is separated from baptism, the celebrant anoints them with chrism immediately after
baptism. 3

[When a great number have been baptised, assisting priests or
deacons may help with the anointing.]

The celebrant first says the following over all the newly baptised
before the anointing.

The God of power and Father of our Lord Jesus Christ
has freed you from sin
and brought you to new life
through water and the Holy Spirit.

He now anoints you with the chrism of salvation,
so that, united with his people,
you may remain for ever a member of Christ
who is Priest, Prophet, and King.

Children:

Amen.

In silence each of the newly baptised is anointed with chrism
on the crown of the head.

Clothing with a Baptismal Garment

The garment used in this rite may be white or of a colour 359
that conforms to local custom. If circumstances suggest, this rite
may be omitted.

The celebrant says the following formulary and at the words 'Receive this baptismal garment' the godparents place the garment
on the newly baptised children.

**N. and N., you have become a new creation
and have clothed yourselves in Christ.
Receive this baptismal garment
and bring it unstained to the judgment seat
    of our Lord Jesus Christ,
so that you may have everlasting life.**

Children:

Amen.

Presentation of a Lighted Candle

297 The celebrant takes the Easter candle in his hands or touches 360
it, saying to the godparents:

**Godparents, please come forward to give to the newly baptised
the light of Christ.**

A godparent of each of the newly baptised goes to the celebrant,
lights a candle from the Easter candle, then presents it to the
newly baptised child.

Then the celebrant says to the children:

**You have been enlightened by Christ.
Walk always as children of the light
and keep the flame of faith alive in your hearts.
When the Lord comes, may you go out to meet him
with all the saints in the heavenly kingdom.**

Children:

Amen.

CELEBRATION OF CONFIRMATION

298 Between the celebration of baptism and confirmation, the assembly may sing a suitable song.

The place for the celebration of confirmation is either at the baptismal font or in the sanctuary, depending on where, according to local conditions, baptism has been celebrated.

If previously baptised children of the catechetical group are to be confirmed, they with their sponsors join the newly baptised children to receive the sacrament.

299 If the bishop has conferred baptism, he should now also confer confirmation. If the bishop is not present, the priest who conferred baptism is authorized to confirm (see no. 284).

[When there are a great many children to be confirmed, the minister of confirmation may associate priests with himself as ministers of the sacrament (see no. 14).]

INVITATION

300 The celebrant first speaks briefly to the children in these or similar words.

My dear children, by your baptism you have been born again in Christ and you have become members of Christ and of his priestly people. Now you are to share in the outpouring of the Holy Spirit among us, the Spirit sent by the Lord upon his apostles at Pentecost and given by them and their successors to the baptised.

The promised strength of the Holy Spirit, which you are to receive, will make you more like Christ and help you to be witnesses to his suffering, death, and resurrection. It will strengthen you to be active members of the Church and to build up the Body of Christ in faith and love.

[The priests who will be associated with the celebrant as ministers of the sacrament now stand next to him.]

With hands joined, the celebrant next addresses the people:

My dear friends, let us pray to God our Father, that he will pour out the Holy Spirit on these children to strengthen them with his gifts and anoint them to be more like Christ, the Son of God.

All pray briefly in silence.

Laying on of Hands

301 The celebrant holds his hands outstretched over the entire group of those to be confirmed and says the following prayer.

[In silence the priests associated as ministers of the sacrament also hold their hands outstretched over the candidates.]

**All-powerful God, Father of our Lord Jesus Christ,
by water and the Holy Spirit
you freed your sons and daughters from sin
and gave them new life.**

**Send your Holy Spirit upon them
to be their helper and guide.**

**Give them the spirit of wisdom and understanding,
the spirit of right judgment and courage,
the spirit of knowledge and reverence.
Fill them with the spirit of wonder and awe in your presence.**

We ask this through Christ our Lord.

R. **Amen.**

Anointing with Chrism

302 A minister brings the chrism to the celebrant.

[When the celebrant is the bishop, priests who are associated as ministers of the sacrament receive the chrism from him.]

Each child to be confirmed, with godparent or godparents, sponsor or sponsors, goes to the celebrant (or to an associated minister of the sacrament); or, if circumstances require, the celebrant (associated ministers) may go to the children.

Either or both godparents or sponsors place the right hand on the shoulder of the child and a godparent or sponsor of each child gives the child's name or the child gives his or her name to the minister of the sacrament. During the conferral of the sacrament an appropriate song may be sung.

The minister of the sacrament dips his right thumb in the chrism and makes the sign of the cross on the forehead of the one to be confirmed as he says:

N., be sealed with the Gift of the Holy Spirit.

Child:

Amen.

The minister of the sacrament adds:

Peace be with you.

Child:

And also with you.

LITURGY OF THE EUCHARIST

303 Since the profession of faith is not said, the general intercessions begin immediately and for the first time the newly baptised children take part in them. Some of the children also take
part in the procession to the altar with the gifts.

304 With Eucharistic Prayers I, II, or III the special interpolations given in the Roman Missal, the ritual Masses, 'Christian
Initiation: Baptism' are used.

Eucharistic Prayer IV with its special interpolation indicated in
the same ritual Masses, may also be used but outside the Easter
Vigil.

305 It is most desirable that the newly baptised children, together
with their godparents, parents, and catechists, receive communion under both kinds.

Before saying 'This is the Lamb of God,' the celebrant may briefly
remind the newly baptised children of the preeminence of the
eucharist, which is the climax of their initiation and the centre
of the whole Christian life.

The celebrant should also pay special attention to any previously baptised children of the catechetical group who at this celebration are to receive communion for the first time. These
children, together with their parents, godparents, sponsors for
confirmation, and catechists, may also receive communion under both kinds.

PERIOD OF POSTBAPTISMAL CATECHESIS OR MYSTAGOGY

The Father chose us to be his adopted children through Jesus Christ

306 A period of postbaptismal catechesis or mystagogy should be pro- ₃₆₉ vided to assist the young neophytes and their companions who have completed their Christian initiation. This period can be arranged by an adaptation of the guidelines given for adults (nos. 234-241).

2 CHRISTIAN INITIATION OF ADULTS IN EXCEPTIONAL CIRCUMSTANCES

He gave power to become children of God to all who believe in his name

307 Exceptional circumstances may arise in which the local bishop, in in-   240
dividual cases, can allow the use of a form of Christian initiation that is
simpler than the usual, complete rite (see no. 34,4).

The bishop may permit this simpler form to consist in the abbreviated form of the rite (nos. 316-345) that is carried out in one celebration.
Or he may permit an expansion of this abbreviated rite, so that there are
celebrations not only of the sacraments of initiation but also of one or more
of the rites belonging to the period of the catechumenate and to the period
of purification and enlightenment (see nos. 308-311).

The extraordinary circumstances in question are either events that
prevent the candidate from completing all the steps of the catechumenate
or a depth of Christian conversion and a degree of religious maturity that
lead the local bishop to decide that the candidate may receive baptism without delay.

EXPANDED FORM

308 Extraordinary circumstances, for example, sickness, old age, change   274
of residence, long absence for travel, may sometimes either prevent a candidate from celebrating the rite of acceptance that leads to the period of
the catechumenate or, having begun the catechumenate, from completing
it by participation in all the rites belonging to the period. Yet merely to
use the abbreviated form of the rite given in nos. 316-345 could mean a
spiritual loss for the candidate, who would be deprived of the benefits of
a longer preparation for the sacraments of initiation. It is therefore important that, with the bishop's permission, an expanded form of initiation
be developed by the incorporation of elements from the complete rite for
the Christian initiation of adults.

309 Through such an expansion of the abbreviated rite a new candidate   275
can reach the same level as those who are already advanced in the catechumenate, since some of the earlier elements from the full rite can be
added, for example, the rite of acceptance into the order of catechumens
(nos. 48-74) or the minor exorcisms (no. 94) and blessings (no. 97) from
the period of the catechumenate. The expansion also makes it possible for
a candidate who had begun the catechumenate with others, but was forced
to interrupt it, to complete the catechumenate alone by celebrating, in

addition to the sacraments of initiation (see nos. 198-210), elements from the full rite, for example, the rite of election (see nos. 105-115) and rites belonging to the period of purification and enlightenment (see nos. 128-136).

310 Parish priests (pastors) can arrange this expanded form of initiation by taking the abbreviated form as a basis, then choosing wisely from the full rite to make adaptations in any of the following ways: 27

> 1. supplementing the abbreviated form: for example, adding rites belonging to the period of the catechumenate (nos. 81-102) or adding the presentations (nos. 144-149; 165-169);
> 2. making the rite of 'Receiving the Candidate' or the 'Liturgy of the Word' in the abbreviated rite separate or expanded celebrations. As to 'Receiving the Candidate' (nos. 316-321), this can be expanded by replacing no. 318 and using elements from the rite of acceptance into the order of catechumens (nos. 48-74); or, depending on the candidate's state of preparation, by celebrating the rite of election (nos. 116-124) in place of nos. 319-320. As to the 'Liturgy of the Word,' after the readings, the intercessions, penitential rite, and prayer of exorcism, nos. 325-327, can be adapted by use of the elements in the scrutinies (nos. 139-141, 153-155, 160-162).
> 3. replacing elements of the complete rite with elements of the abbreviated form; or combining the rite of acceptance into the order of catechumens (nos. 48-74) and the rite of election (nos. 116-124) at the time of receiving a properly disposed candidate (which is comparable to the time of receiving interested inquirers in the period of the precatechumenate; see no. 39,3).

311 When this expanded form of initiation is arranged, care should be taken to ensure that: 27

> 1. the candidate has received a full catechesis;
> 2. the rite is celebrated with the active participation of an assembly;
> 3. after receiving the sacraments the neophyte has the benefit of a period of postbaptismal catechesis, if at all possible.

Abbreviated Form

312 Before the abbreviated form of the rite is celebrated the candidate must have gone through an adequate period of instruction and preparation before baptism, in order to purify his or her motives for requesting baptism and to grow stronger in conversion and faith. The candidate should also have chosen godparents or a godparent (see no. 11) and become acquainted with the local Christian community (see nos. 39 and 75,2). 24

313 This rite includes elements that express the presentation and welcoming of the candidate and that also express the candidate's clear and firm re- 24

solve to request Christian initiation, as well as the Church's approval of the candidate. A suitable liturgy of the word is also celebrated, then the sacraments of initiation.

314 Normally the rite is celebrated within Mass. The choice of readings should be in keeping with the character of the celebration; they may be either those of the day or those in the Lectionary for Mass: ritual Mass, 'Christian Initiation apart from the Easter Vigil' (Vol. III, pp. 18-47). The other Mass texts are those of one of the ritual Masses 'Christian Initiation: Baptism' (Vol. III, pp. 59-73) or of another suitable Mass. After receiving baptism and confirmation, the candidate takes part for the first time in the celebration of the eucharist. 243

315 If at all possible, the celebration should take place on a Sunday (see no. 27), with the local community taking an active part. 244

OUTLINE OF THE RITE

RECEIVING THE CANDIDATE

Greeting
Opening Dialogue
Candidate's Declaration
Affirmation by the Godparents
Invitation to the Celebration of the Word of God

LITURGY OF THE WORD

Readings
Homily
Intercessions for the Candidate
[Penitential Rite]
Prayer of Exorcism
Anointing with the Oil of Catechumens
  or Laying on of Hands

CELEBRATION OF BAPTISM

Invitation to Prayer
Prayer over the Water
Profession of Faith
    Renunciation of Sin
    Profession of Faith
Baptism
Explanatory Rites
    [Clothing with a Baptismal Garment]
    Presentation of a Lighted Candle

CELEBRATION OF CONFIRMATION

Invitation
Laying on of Hands
Anointing with Chrism

LITURGY OF THE EUCHARIST

CHRISTIAN INITIATION OF ADULTS IN EXCEPTIONAL CIRCUMSTANCES
(Abbreviated Form)

RECEIVING THE CANDIDATE

316 Before the celebration begins, the candidate with his or her
godparents and friends waits outside the church or inside, at the
entrance or some other convenient place. The celebrant, wearing the vestments for Mass, goes to meet them, as the faithful
sing a psalm or another suitable song.

245

GREETING

317 The celebrant greets the candidate in a friendly manner.
He speaks to the candidate, godparents, and friends, pointing
out the joy and happiness of the Church. He recalls for the godparents and friends the particular experience and religious response that have led the candidate, following his or her own
spiritual path, to the present celebration.

246

The celebrant then invites the godparents and the candidate to
come forward. As they are taking their place before him, an appropriate song may be sung, for example, Psalm 62(63):1-8.

OPENING DIALOGUE

318 Facing the candidate, the celebrant asks the questions that
follow. In asking about the candidate's intention he may use words
other than those provided and may let the candidate answer in
his or her own words: for example, to the first question, 'What
do you ask of the Church of God?' or 'What do you desire?' or
'For what reason have you come?', he may receive such answers
as 'The grace of Christ' or 'Entrance into the Church' or 'Eternal life' or other suitable responses. The celebrant will phrase
his next question according to the answer received.

247

Celebrant:

What do you ask of God's Church?

Candidate:

Faith.

Celebrant:

What does faith offer you?

Candidate:

Eternal life.

CANDIDATE'S DECLARATION

319 The celebrant addresses the candidate, adapting as required the following or similar words to the answers received in the opening dialogue.

This is eternal life: to know the one true God and Jesus Christ, whom he has sent. Christ has been raised from the dead and appointed by God as the Lord of life and ruler of all things, seen and unseen.

You would not ask for this life or seek baptism today, unless you had already come to know Christ and wanted to become his disciple. And I ask you, have you listened to Christ's word and resolved to keep his commandments? Have you shared our way of life and joined with us in prayer? Have you done all these things with the intention of becoming a Christian?

Candidate:

I have.

AFFIRMATION BY THE GODPARENTS

320 Then the celebrant turns to the godparents and asks:

You are the candidate's godparents. As God is your witness, do you consider him/her worthy to be admitted today to the sacraments of Christian initiation?

Godparents:

I do.

Celebrant:

You have spoken in N.'s favour. Are you prepared to help him/her to serve Christ by your words and example?

Godparents:

I am.

The celebrant, with hands joined, says:

250

Let us pray.

Father of mercy,
we thank you for your servant, N.
You have sought and summoned him/her in many ways
and he/she has turned to seek you.

You have called him/her today
and he/she has answered in the presence of the Church.

Look favourably upon him/her
and let your loving purpose be fulfiled within him/her.

We ask this through Christ our Lord.

R. Amen.

INVITATION TO THE CELEBRATION OF THE WORD OF GOD

321 Using the following or similar words, accompanied by an appropriate gesture, the celebrant invites the candidate and the godparents to enter the church.

251

Celebrant:

N., come into the church,
to share with us at the table of God's word.

During the entrance a suitable song is sung or the following antiphon, with Psalm 33(34):2, 3, 6, 9, 10.

Come, my children, and listen to me;
I will teach you the fear of the Lord.

LITURGY OF THE WORD

322 When the candidate and the godparents have taken their place in the church and the celebrant has reached the sanctuary, the liturgy of the word begins; the usual introductory rites of the Mass are omitted.

READINGS

323 The readings are those already indicated in no. 314 (Lectionary for Mass, Vol. III, p. 47, which simply cross-refers to Vol. III, pp. 65-73).

HOMILY

324 The homily follows the gospel reading.

INTERCESSIONS FOR THE CANDIDATE

325 After the homily, the candidate and the godparents come before the celebrant. The entire assembly joins in offering the following or similar intercessions.

Celebrant:

Let us pray for our brother/sister who asks for Christ's sacraments, and let us pray for ourselves, sinners that we are, that we may all draw nearer to Christ in faith and repentance and walk untiringly in newness of life.

Assisting minister:

That the Lord may kindle in all of us a spirit of true repentance, let us pray to the Lord:

R. Lord, hear our prayer.

Assisting minister:

That we, who have died to sin and been saved by Christ through baptism, may be living proof of his grace, let us pray to the Lord:

R. Lord, hear our prayer.

Assisting minister:

That with trust in God's love and sorrow for sin our brother/sister may prepare to meet Christ his/her Saviour, let us pray to the Lord:

R. Lord, hear our prayer.

Assisting minister:

That by following Christ, who takes away the sin of the world, our brother/sister may be healed of the infection of sin and freed from its power, let us pray to the Lord:

R. Lord, hear our prayer.

Assisting minister:

That by the power of the Holy Spirit he/she may be cleansed from sin and guided along the paths of holiness, let us pray to the Lord:

R. Lord, hear our prayer.

Assisting minister:

That through burial with Christ in baptism he/she may die to sin and live always for God, let us pray to the Lord:

R. Lord, hear our prayer.

Assisting minister:

That on the day of judgment he/she may come before the Father bearing fruits of holiness and love, let us pray to the Lord:

R. Lord, hear our prayer.

Assisting minister:

That the entire world, for which the Father gave his beloved Son, may believe in his love and turn to him, let us pray to the Lord:

R. Lord, hear our prayer.

PENITENTIAL RITE

326 The penitential rite may be omitted, as circumstances suggest. When it is celebrated, after the intercessions the candidate bows his or her head or kneels and joins the assembly in reciting the general confession of sins.

254

I confess to almighty God,
and to you, my brothers and sisters,
that I have sinned through my own fault

> All strike their breast.

in my thoughts and in my words,
in what I have done,
and in what I have failed to do;
and I ask blessed Mary, ever-virgin,
all the angels and saints,
and you, my brothers and sisters,
to pray for me to the Lord our God.

The absolution 'May almighty God' is not said.

Prayer of Exorcism

327 The celebrant concludes the intercessions (and penitential rite) with the following prayer.

Father of mercies,
you sent your only Son
to rescue us from the slavery of sin
and to give us freedom as your children.

We pray for your servant N.;
he/she has faced the temptations of this world
and been tested by the cunning of Satan;
now he/she acknowledges his/her sinfulness
and professes his/her faith.

By the passion and resurrection of your Son
deliver him/her from the powers of darkness
and strengthen him/her through the grace of Christ,
that he/she may journey through life,
    shielded by your unfailing care.

We ask this through Christ our Lord.

R. Amen.

328 The celebrant continues immediately with the anointing of the candidate with the oil of catechumens, option A. But if by decision of the conference of bishops this anointing is to be omitted (see no. 33,7), the celebrant continues with a laying on of hands, option B.

256

A   ANOINTING WITH THE OIL OF CATECHUMENS: The celebrant faces the candidate and says:

We anoint you with the oil of salvation
in the name of Christ our Saviour.
May he strengthen you with his power,
who lives and reigns for ever and ever.

Candidate:

Amen.

The candidate is anointed with the oil of catechumens on the breast or on both hands or even on other parts of the body, if this seems desirable.

B   LAYING ON OF HANDS: The celebrant faces the candidate and says:

May Christ our Saviour
strengthen you with his power,
for he is Lord for ever and ever.

Candidate:

Amen.

Then, in silence, the celebrant lays hands on the candidate.

CELEBRATION OF BAPTISM

INVITATION TO PRAYER

329 The candidate with the godparent or the godparents goes to the baptismal font with the celebrant, then the celebrant addresses the following or a similar invitation for the assembly to join in prayer for the candidate.

257

Dear friends, let us pray to almighty God for our brother/sister N., who is asking for baptism. He has called N. and brought him/her to this moment; may he grant N. light and strength to follow Christ with a resolute heart and to profess the faith of the Church. May he give N. the new life of the Holy Spirit, whom we are about to call down on this water.

Prayer over the Water

> 330 Next, the celebrant blesses the water, using option A; he may also use one of the other blessing formularies given in no. 215 as options B and C.
>
> But when baptism is celebrated during the Easter season and water already blessed at the Easter Vigil is available, the celebrant uses option B, so that this part of the celebration will retain the themes of thanksgiving and intercession; he may also use the second Easter-season thanksgiving formulary given in no. 215 as option E.

A
> Blessing of the Water: Facing the font (or vessel) containing the water, the celebrant says the following (music, p. 126).

Father,
you give us grace through sacramental signs,
which tell us of the wonders of your unseen power.

In baptism we use your gift of water,
which you have made a rich symbol of the grace
you give us in this sacrament.

At the very dawn of creation
your Spirit breathed on the waters,
making them the wellspring of all holiness.

The waters of the great flood
you made a sign of the waters of baptism
that make an end of sin
and a new beginning of goodness.

Through the waters of the Red Sea
you led Israel out of slavery
to be an image of God's holy people,
set free from sin by baptism.

In the waters of the Jordan
your Son was baptised by John
and anointed with the Spirit.

Your Son willed that water and blood should flow from his side
as he hung upon the cross.

After his resurrection he told his disciples:
'Go out and teach all nations,
baptising them in the name of the Father, and of the Son,
    and of the Holy Spirit.'

Father,
look now with love upon your Church
and unseal for it the fountain of baptism.

By the power of the Holy Spirit
give to this water the grace of your Son,
so that in the sacrament of baptism
all those whom you have created in your likeness
may be cleansed from sin
and rise to a new birth of innocence
by water and the Holy Spirit.

> Before continuing, the celebrant pauses and touches the water
> with his right hand.

We ask you, Father, with your Son
to send the Holy Spirit upon the waters of this font.
May all who are buried with Christ in the death of baptism
rise also with him to newness of life.

We ask this through Christ our Lord.

> All:

Amen.

B

EASTER-SEASON THANKSGIVING OVER BLESSED WATER: Facing the
font (or vessel) containing the blessed water, the celebrant says
the following.

389

Praise to you, almighty God and Father,
for you have created water to cleanse and to give life.

> All sing or say the following or another suitable acclamation.

Blessed be God.

Praise to you, Lord Jesus Christ, the Father's only Son,
for you offered yourself on the cross,
that in the blood and water flowing from your side
and through your death and resurrection
the Church might be born.

All:

Blessed be God.

Celebrant:

Praise to you, God the Holy Spirit,
for you anointed Christ at his baptism in the waters
    of the Jordan,
that we might all be baptised in you.

All:

Blessed be God.

The celebrant then concludes with the following prayer.

You have called your children, N. and N., to this cleansing water,
that they may share in the faith of your Church
    and have eternal life.
By the mystery of this consecrated water
lead them to a new and spiritual birth.
We ask this through Christ our Lord.

All:

Amen.

PROFESSION OF FAITH

331 After the blessing of the water (or prayer of thanksgiving),
the celebrant continues with the profession of faith, which includes the renunciation of sin and the profession itself (between
which there may be the anointing).

RENUNCIATION OF SIN

332 Using one of the following formularies, the celebrant questions the candidate.

[If circumstances require, the conference of bishops may make the three formularies more specific and detailed, especially in regions where it is necessary for the candidates to reject superstitious and magical practises (see no. 72).]

A   Celebrant:
Do you reject sin so as to live in the freedom of God's children?

Candidate:
I do.

Celebrant:
Do you reject the glamour of evil, and refuse to be mastered by sin?

Candidate:
I do.

Celebrant:
Do you reject Satan, father of sin and prince of darkness?

Candidate:
I do.

B   Celebrant:
Do you reject Satan, and all his works, and all his empty promises?

Candidate:
I do.

C   Celebrant:
Do you reject Satan?

Candidate:
I do.

Celebrant:
And all his works?

Candidate:
I do.

Celebrant:

And all his empty promises?

Candidate:

I do.

Profession of Faith

333 Then the celebrant asks the candidate:

**N., do you believe in God, the Father almighty,
creator of heaven and earth?**

Candidate:

I do.

Celebrant:

**Do you believe in Jesus Christ, his only Son, our Lord,
who was born of the Virgin Mary,
was crucified, died, and was buried,
rose from the dead,
and is now seated at the right hand of the Father?**

Candidate:

I do.

Celebrant:

**Do you believe in the Holy Spirit,
the holy catholic Church, the communion of saints,
the forgiveness of sins, the resurrection of the body,
and the life everlasting?**

Candidate:

I do.

Baptism

334 Immediately after the profession of faith the celebrant baptises the candidate either by immersion, option A, or by the pouring of water, option B. After the baptism it is appropriate for the people to sing a short acclamation (Appendix, no. 452).

A

If baptism is by immersion, of the whole body or of the head only, decency and decorum should be preserved. Either or both godparents touch the candidate. The celebrant, immersing the candidate's whole body or head three times, baptises the candidate in the name of the Trinity.

261

N., I baptise you in the name of the Father,

He immerses the candidate the first time.

and of the Son,

He immerses the candidate the second time.

and of the Holy Spirit.

He immerses the candidate the third time.

B

If baptism is by the pouring of water, either or both godparents place the right hand on the shoulder of the candidate, and the celebrant, taking baptismal water and pouring it three times on the candidate's bowed head, baptises the candidate in the name of the Trinity.

262

N., I baptise you in the name of the Father,

He pours water the first time.

and of the Son,

He pours water the second time.

and of the Holy Spirit.

He pours water the third time.

Explanatory Rites

335 The celebration of baptism proceeds immediately with the explanatory rites, after which the celebration of confirmation follows.

Clothing with a Baptismal Garment

336 The garment used in this rite may be white or of a colour that conforms to local custom. If circumstances suggest, this rite may be omitted.

264

The celebrant says the following formulary, and at the words 'Receive this baptismal garment' the godparent or godparents place the garment on the newly baptised.

N., you have become a new creation
and have clothed yourself in Christ.
Receive this baptismal garment
and bring it unstained to the judgment seat
   of our Lord Jesus Christ,
so that you may have everlasting life.

Newly baptised:

Amen.

PRESENTATION OF A LIGHTED CANDLE

337 The celebrant takes the Easter candle in his hands or touches it, saying to the godparent(s):

Please come forward to give to the newly baptised the light of Christ.

A godparent goes to the celebrant and lights a candle from the Easter candle, then presents it to the newly baptised.

Then the celebrant says to the newly baptised:

You have been enlightened by Christ.
Walk always as children of the light
and keep the flame of faith alive in your hearts.
When the Lord comes, may you go out to meet him
with all the saints in the heavenly kingdom.

Newly baptised:

Amen.

CELEBRATION OF CONFIRMATION

338 Between the celebration of baptism and confirmation, the assembly may sing an appropriate song.

339 If the bishop is not present, the celebrant who conferred baptism confers confirmation.

340 The celebrant first speaks briefly to the person newly baptised in these or similar words.

268

N., born again in Christ by baptism, you have become a member of Christ and of his priestly people. Now you are to share in the outpouring of the Holy Spirit among us, the Spirit sent by the Lord upon his apostles at Pentecost and given by them and their successors to the baptised.

The promised strength of the Holy Spirit, which you are to receive, will make you more like Christ and help you to be a witness to his suffering, death, and resurrection. It will strengthen you to be an active member of the Church and to build up the Body of Christ in faith and love.

With hands joined, the celebrant next addresses the people:

My dear friends, let us pray to God our Father, that he will pour out the Holy Spirit on our newly baptised brother/sister to strengthen him/her with his gifts and anoint him/her to be more like Christ, the Son of God.

All pray briefly in silence.

LAYING ON OF HANDS

341 The celebrant then lays hands on the person to be confirmed and says the following prayer.

269

All-powerful God, Father of our Lord Jesus Christ,
by water and the Holy Spirit ·
you freed your son/daughter from sin
and gave him/her new life.

Send your Holy Spirit upon him/her
to be his/her helper and guide.

Give him/her the spirit of wisdom and understanding,
the spirit of right judgment and courage,
the spirit of knowledge and reverence.
Fill him/her with the spirit of wonder and awe in your presence.

We ask this through Christ our Lord.

R. Amen.

342 A minister brings the chrism to the celebrant.

The candidate, with the godparents, goes to the celebrant. Either or both godparents place the right hand on the shoulder of the candidate and either a godparent or the candidate gives the candidate's name to the celebrant. During the conferral of the sacrament an appropriate song may be sung.

The celebrant dips his right thumb in the chrism and makes the sign of the cross on the forehead of the one to be confirmed as he says:

N., be sealed with the Gift of the Holy Spirit.

Newly confirmed:
Amen.

The celebrant adds:
Peace be with you.

Newly confirmed:
And also with you.

LITURGY OF THE EUCHARIST

343 Since the profession of faith is not said, the general intercessions begin immediately and for the first time the neophyte takes part in them. He or she also helps to carry the gifts when they are brought to the altar.

344 The eucharistic prayer is to include the special interpolations given for Eucharistic Prayers I, II, III, and IV in the Roman Missal, ritual Masses, 'Christian Initiation: Baptism.'

345 It is most desirable that the neophyte, together with his or her godparents, parents, spouse, and catechists, receive communion under both kinds.

Before saying 'This is the Lamb of God' the celebrant may briefly remind the neophyte of the preeminence of the eucharist, which is the climax of Christian initiation and the centre of the whole Christian life.

3 CHRISTIAN INITIATION OF A PERSON IN DANGER OF DEATH

By becoming coheirs with Christ, we share in his sufferings;
we will also share in his glory

346 Persons, whether catechumens or not, who are in danger of death but are not at the point of death and so are able to hear and answer the questions involved may be baptised with this short rite.   278

347 Persons who have already been accepted as catechumens must make a promise that upon recovery they will complete the usual catechesis. Persons who are not catechumens must give serious indication of their conversion to Christ and renunciation of pagan worship and must not be seen to be attached to anything that conflicts with the moral life (for example, 'simultaneous polygamy'). They must also promise that upon recovery they will go through the complete programme of initiation as it applies to them.   279

348 This shorter rite is designed particularly for use by catechists and lay-persons; a priest or a deacon may use it in a case of emergency. But normally a priest or a deacon is to use the abbreviated form of Christian initiation given in nos. 316-345, making any changes required by circumstances of place and time.   280

    The minister of baptism who is a priest should, when the chrism is at hand and there is time, confer confirmation after the baptism; in this case there is no postbaptismal anointing.

    The minister of baptism who is a priest, a deacon, or a catechist or lay-person having permission to distribute communion should, if this is possible, give the eucharist to the newly baptised person. In this case before the beginning of the celebration of the rite the blessed sacrament is placed reverently on a table covered with a white cloth.

349 In the case of a person who is at the point of death, that is, whose death is imminent, and time is short, the minister, omitting everything else, pours natural water (even if not blessed) on the head of the sick person, while saying the usual sacramental form (see *Christian Initiation*, General Introduction, no. 23).   281

350 If persons who were baptised when in danger of death or at the point of death recover their health, they are to be given a suitable formation, be welcomed at the church in due time, and there receive the other sacraments of initiation. In such cases the guidelines given in nos. 376-386 for baptised but uncatechized adults are followed, with the necessary changes. The same guidelines should be applied when sick persons recover after receiving not only baptism but also confirmation and eucharist as viaticum.   282 294

OUTLINE OF THE RITE

INTRODUCTORY RITES

Opening Dialogue
Affirmation by the Godparent and Witnesses

LITURGY OF THE WORD

Gospel Reading
Intercessions for the Candidate
Prayer over the Candidate

CELEBRATION OF BAPTISM

Renunciation of Sin
Profession of Faith
Baptism
[Anointing after Baptism]

CELEBRATION OF CONFIRMATION

Invitation
Laying on of Hands
Anointing with Chrism

CELEBRATION OF VIATICUM

Invitation to Prayer
Communion as Viaticum
Prayer after Communion

CONCLUDING RITES

Blessing
Sign of Peace

CHRISTIAN INITIATION OF A PERSON IN DANGER OF DEATH

283

351 The minister greets the family and then speaks with the sick person about his or her request for baptism and, if the sick person is not a catechumen, about his or her reasons for conversion. After deciding to baptise him or her, the minister should, if necessary, instruct the person briefly.

284

352 Then the minister invites the family, the person designated as godparent, and the friends and neigbours present to gather around the sick person and selects one or two of those present as witnesses. Water, even if it is not blessed, is prepared.

INTRODUCTORY RITES

Opening Dialogue

285

353 The minister addresses the sick person in these or similar words.

Dear brother/sister, you have asked to be baptised because you wish to have eternal life. This is eternal life: to know the one, true God and Jesus Christ, whom he has sent. This is the faith of Christians. Do you acknowledge this?

Candidate:

I do.

Minister:

As well as professing your faith in Jesus Christ, you must also be willing to follow his commands, as Christians do. Are you willing to accept this?

Candidate:

I am.

Minister:

Are you prepared to live as Christians do?

Candidate:

I am.

Minister:

Promise, therefore, that once you have recovered your strength, you will try to know Christ better and follow a course of Christian formation. Do you so promise?

Candidate:

I do.

AFFIRMATION BY THE GODPARENT AND WITNESSES

354 Turning to the godparent and to the witnesses, the minister asks them the following questions in these or similar words.

You have heard N.'s promise. As his/her godparent do you promise to remind him/her of it and to help him/her to learn the teaching of Christ, to take part in the life of our community, and to bear witness as a true Christian?

Godparent:

I do.

Minister:

And will the rest of you, who have witnessed this promise, assist him/her in fulfilling it?

Witnesses:

We will.

Then the minister turns to the sick person and says:

Therefore you will now be baptised into eternal life, in accordance with the command of our Lord Jesus Christ.

LITURGY OF THE WORD

GOSPEL READING

355 According to time and circumstances, the minister reads some words from a gospel and explains them. One of the following may be used (see Appendix 3, no. 455, for texts in full).

1   Matthew 22:35-40 (Lectionary, Vol. III, p. 65)
     —*This is the greatest and the first commandment.*
2   Matthew 28:18-20 (Vol. III, p. 66)
     —*Make disciples of all the nations; baptise them in the name of the Father and of the Son and of the Holy Spirit.*
3   Mark 1:9-11 (Vol. III, p. 66)
     —*He was baptised in the Jordan by John.*
4   John 3:1-6 (Vol. III, p. 68)
     —*Unless a man is born from above, he cannot see the kingdom of heaven.*
5   John 6:44-47 (Vol. III, p. 70)
     —*Everybody who believes has eternal life.*

INTERCESSIONS FOR THE CANDIDATE

288

356 The minister may adapt or shorten the intercessions according to the condition of the sick person. The intercessions may be omitted if the sick person appears to be tiring. The minister begins:

Let us pray to the God of mercy for our sick brother/sister who has asked for the gift of baptism; let us pray for his/her godparent and for all his/her family and friends.

Assisting minister:

Father, increase his/her faith in Christ, your Son and our Saviour; in faith we make our prayer:

℟. Lord, hear us.

Assisting minister:

Grant his/her desire to have eternal life and enter the kingdom of heaven; in faith we make our prayer:

℟. Lord, hear us.

Assisting minister:

Fulfil his/her hope of knowing you, the Creator of the world and the Father of all; in faith we make our prayer:

℟. Lord, hear us.

Assisting minister:

Through baptism forgive his/her sins and make him/her holy; in faith we make our prayer:

℟. Lord, hear us.

Assisting minister:

Grant him/her the salvation that Christ won by his death and resurrection; in faith we make our prayer:

℟. Lord, hear us.

In your love adopt him/her into your family; in faith we make our prayer:

R. Lord, hear us.

[Assisting minister:
Restore him/her to health so that he/she may have the time to know and imitate Christ more perfectly; in faith we make our prayer:

R. Lord, hear us.]

Assisting minister:
Keep united in faith and love all who have been baptised into the one Body of Christ; in faith we make our prayer:

R. Lord, hear us.

PRAYER OVER THE CANDIDATE

357 The minister concludes the intercessions with the following prayer.

Father,
look kindly upon the faith and longing of your servant N.;
through this water
by which you have chosen to give us birth from above,
join him/her to Christ's death and resurrection.

Forgive all his/her sins,
adopt him/her as your own,
and count him/her among your holy people.

[Grant also that he/she may be restored to health,
to render you thanks in your Church
and grow in faithfulness to the teaching of Christ.]

We ask this through Christ our Lord.

R. Amen.

CELEBRATION OF BAPTISM

RENUNCIATION OF SIN

290

358 The minister first asks the sick person to renounce sin. The minister may use the following formulary or the longer formulary given in no. 332 and may make pertinent adaptations (see no. 72).

Minister:

Do you reject Satan,
and all his works,
and all his empty promises?

Candidate:

I do.

PROFESSION OF FAITH

290

359 A profession of faith is then made. One of the following formularies may be used.

A
    Minister:

N., do you believe in God, the Father almighty,
    creator of heaven and earth?

Candidate:

I do.

Minister:

Do you believe in Jesus Christ, his only Son, our Lord,
    who was born of the Virgin Mary,
    was crucified, died, and was buried,
    rose from the dead,
    and is now seated at the right hand of the Father?

Candidate:

I do.

Minister:

Do you believe in the Holy Spirit,
    the holy catholic Church, the communion of saints,
    the forgiveness of sins, the resurrection of the body,
    and the life everlasting?

Candidate:

I do.

B   Candidate:

I believe in God, the Father almighty,
    creator of heaven and earth.

I believe in Jesus Christ, his only Son, our Lord.
    He was conceived by the power of the Holy Spirit
        and born of the Virgin Mary.
    He suffered under Pontius Pilate,
        was crucified, died, and was buried.
    He descended to the dead.
    On the third day he rose again.
    He ascended into heaven,
        and is seated at the right hand of the Father.
    He will come again to judge the living and the dead.

I believe in the Holy Spirit,
    the holy catholic Church,
    the communion of saints,
    the forgiveness of sins,
    the resurrection of the body,
    and the life everlasting. Amen.

Baptism

360 The minister, using the name the sick person desires to have,
baptises him or her, saying:

N., I baptise you in the name of the Father,

The minister pours water the first time.

and of the Son,

The minister pours water the second time.

and of the Holy Spirit.

The minister pours water the third time.

361 If the minister of baptism is a deacon, he says the following   292
prayer, then in silence anoints the newly baptised with chrism
on the crown of the head.

The God of power and Father of our Lord Jesus Christ
has freed you from sin
and brought you to new life
through water and the Holy Spirit.

He now anoints you with the chrism of salvation,
so that, united with his people,
you may remain for ever a member of Christ
who is Priest, Prophet, and King.

Newly baptised:

Amen.

362 If the minister is not a priest, the rite continues with the
celebration of viaticum (no. 369).

363 If neither confirmation nor viaticum will be celebrated, one
of the alternative concluding rites (no. 375) follows baptism.

CELEBRATION OF CONFIRMATION

364 If the minister of baptism is a priest, he should also confer   293
confirmation.

If there is not sufficient time because of the condition of the sick
person, the 'Invitation' (no. 365) may be omitted; it is enough
for the priest to anoint with chrism, while saying the words 'N.
be sealed, . . .'; if possible he first lays hands on the sick person
with the prayer 'All-powerful God.'

INVITATION

365 The priest first speaks briefly to the newly baptised in the   293
following or similar words.

N., born again in Christ by baptism, you have become a member of Christ and of his priestly people. Now you are to share in the outpouring of the Holy Spirit among us, the Spirit sent by the Lord upon his apostles at Pentecost and given by them and their successors to the baptised.

> All pray in silence for a short time.

LAYING ON OF HANDS

> **366** The priest lays hands on the newly baptised and says the following prayer.

All-powerful God, Father of our Lord Jesus Christ,
by water and the Holy Spirit
you freed your son/daughter from sin
and gave him/her new life.

Send your Holy Spirit upon him/her
to be his/her helper and guide.

Give him/her the spirit of wisdom and understanding,
the spirit of right judgment and courage,
the spirit of knowledge and reverence.
Fill him/her with the spirit of wonder and awe in your presence.

We ask this through Christ our Lord.

℟. **Amen.**

ANOINTING WITH CHRISM

> **367** The priest dips his right thumb in the chrism and makes the sign of the cross on the forehead of the one to be confirmed as he says:

N., be sealed with the Gift of the Holy Spirit.

> Newly confirmed:

Amen.

> The priest adds:

Peace be with you.

> Newly confirmed:

And also with you.

368 If viaticum will not be celebrated, one of the alternative concluding rites (no. 375) follows confirmation.

CELEBRATION OF VIATICUM

369 Communion as viaticum is given immediately after confirmation or, if confirmation is not celebrated, immediately after the celebration of baptism.

294

INVITATION TO PRAYER

370 The minister addresses the sick person: if viaticum follows the celebration of confirmation, the minister uses option A or similar words; if confirmation is not celebrated and viaticum follows baptism, the minister uses option B or similar words.

A   N., God our Father has freed you from your sins, has given you   294
a new birth and made you his son/daughter in Christ. Before you partake of the body of the Lord and in the spirit of that adoption which you have received today, join us now in praying as our Lord himself taught us.

Then the sick person and all present join the minister in the Lord's Prayer.

Our Father . . .

B   N., God our Father has freed you from your sins, has given you   294
a new birth and made you his son/daughter in Christ. Soon, God willing, you will receive the fulness of the Holy Spirit through confirmation. Before you partake of the body of the Lord and in the spirit of that adoption which you have received today, join us now in praying as our Lord himself taught us.

Then the sick person and all present join the minister in the Lord's Prayer.

Our Father . . .

Communion as Viaticum

371 The minister shows the eucharistic bread to those present, using one of the following formularies.

A   Jesus Christ is the food for our journey;
he calls us to the heavenly table.

B   This is the Lamb of God
who takes away the sins of the world.
Happy are those who are called to his supper.

The sick person and all who are to receive communion say:
**Lord, I am not worthy to receive you,
but only say the word and I shall be healed.**

The minister goes to the sick person and, showing the blessed sacrament, says:
The body of Christ.

The sick person answers:
Amen.

Then the minister says:
The blood of Christ.

The sick person answers:
Amen.

Immediately, or after giving communion to the sick person, the minister adds the form for viaticum.

**May the Lord Jesus Christ protect you
and lead you to eternal life.**

The sick person answers:
Amen.

Others present who wish to receive communion then do so in the usual way.

A short period of silent prayer may follow.

PRAYER AFTER COMMUNION

372 The minister says a concluding prayer.

Let us pray.

Pause for silent prayer, if this has not preceded.

Father,
almighty and eternal God,
our brother/sister has received the eucharist
with faith in you and in your healing power.
May the body and blood of Christ
bring him/her eternal healing in mind and body.

We ask this in the name of Jesus the Lord.

R. **Amen.**

CONCLUDING RITES

BLESSING

373 The minister blesses the sick person and the others present, using one of the following blessings.

A   A minister who is a priest or deacon says:

May the Lord be with you to protect you.

R. **Amen.**

May the Lord guide you and give you strength.

R. **Amen.**

May the Lord watch over you, keep you in his care,
and bless you with his peace.

R. **Amen.**

May almighty God bless you,
the Father, and the Son, ✠ and the Holy Spirit.

R. **Amen.**

B   A lay minister invokes God's blessing and signs himself or her-
           self with the sign of the cross, saying:

**May the Lord bless us,
protect us from all evil,
and bring us to everlasting life.**

R. **Amen.**

SIGN OF PEACE

374 The minister and the others present may then give the sick
person the sign of peace.

ALTERNATIVE CONCLUDING RITES

375 When the celebration is concluded after confirmation and
viaticum is not given, the rite is concluded by use of option A.
When the celebration concludes immediately after baptism and
neither confirmation nor viaticum is celebrated, the rite is concluded by use of option B.

A   The minister addresses the sick person in the following words.

**N., God our Father has freed you from your sins, has given you
a new birth and made you his son/daughter in Christ. Soon,
God willing, you will approach the altar of God to share the
food of life at the table of his sacrifice. In the spirit of that adoption which you have received today, join us now in praying as
our Lord himself taught us.**

Then the sick person and all present join the minister in saying:

Our Father . . .

The blessing (no. 373) and sign of peace (no. 374) may then be
given.

B   The minister addresses the sick person in the following words.

**N., God our Father has freed you from your sins, has given you
a new birth and made you his son/daughter in Christ. Soon,
God willing, you will receive the fulness of the Holy Spirit**

through confirmation and will approach the altar of God to share the food of life at the table of his sacrifice. In the spirit of that adoption which you have received today, join us now in praying as our Lord himself taught us.

Then the sick person and all present join the minister in saying:

Our Father . . .

The blessing (no. 373) and sign of peace (no. 374) may then be given.

4 PREPARATION OF UNCATECHIZED ADULTS FOR CONFIRMATION AND EUCHARIST

If then you have been raised with Christ, seek the things that are above, where Christ is seated at the right hand of God

376 The following pastoral guidelines concern adults who were baptised 295 as infants but did not receive further catechetical formation nor, consequently, the sacraments of confirmation and eucharist. These suggestions may also be applied to similar cases, especially that of an adult who recovers after being baptised in danger of death or at the point of death (see no. 350).

Even though uncatechized adults have not yet heard the message of the mystery of Christ, their status differs from that of catechumens, since by baptism they have already become members of the Church and children of God. Hence their conversion is based on the baptism they have already received, the effects of which they must develop.

377 As in the case of catechumens, the preparation of these adults requires 296 a considerable time (see no. 76), during which the faith infused in baptism must grow in them and take deep root through the pastoral formation they receive. A programme of training, catechesis suited to their needs, contact with the community of the faithful, and participation in certain liturgical rites are needed in order to strengthen them in the Christian life.

378 For the most part the plan of catechesis corresponds to the one laid 297 down for catechumens (see no. 75,1). But in the process of catechesis the priest, deacon, or catechist should take into account that these adults have a special status because they are already baptised.

379 Just as it helps catechumens, the Christian community should also 298 help these adults by its love and prayer (see nos. 4 and 75,2) and by testifying to their suitability when it is time for them to be admitted to the sacraments (see nos. 107, 108).

380 A sponsor presents these adults to the community (see no. 10). During the period of their catechetical formation, they all choose godparents 299 (a godfather, a godmother, or both) approved by the priest. Their godparents work with these adults as the representatives of the community and have the same responsibilities as the godparents have toward catechumens (see no. 11). The same persons who were the godparents at the baptism of these adults may be chosen as godparents at this time, provided they are truly capable of carrying out the responsibilities of godparents.

381 The period of preparation is made holy by means of liturgical celebra- 300 tions. The first of these is a rite by which the adults are welcomed into

the community and acknowledge themselves to be part of it because they have already been marked with the seal of baptism.

382 Once a rite of reception has been celebrated, these adults take part in celebrations of the word of God, both those of the entire Christian assembly and those celebrations arranged specially for the benefit of the catechumens (see nos. 81-84).

383 As a sign of God's activity in this work of preparation, some of the rites belonging to the catechumenate, especially suited to the condition and spiritual needs of these baptised adults, can be used to advantage. Among these are the presentation of the Creed (nos. 144-149) and of the Lord's Prayer (nos. 165-169) or also a presentation of a book of the Gospels (no. 64).

384 The period of catechesis for these adults should be properly coordinated with the liturgical year. This is particularly true of its final phase, which should as a rule coincide with Lent. During the Lenten season penitential services should be arranged in such a way as to prepare these adults for the celebration of the sacrament of penance.

385 The high point of their entire formation will normally be the Easter Vigil. At that time they will make a profession of the faith in which they were baptised, receive the sacrament of confirmation, and take part in the eucharist. If, because neither the bishop nor another authorized minister is present, confirmation cannot be given at the Easter Vigil, it is to be celebrated as soon as possible and, if this can be arranged, during the Easter season.

386 These adults will complete their Christian formation and become fully integrated into the community by going through the period of postbaptismal catechesis or mystagogy with the newly baptised members of the Christian community.

5 RECEPTION OF BAPTISED CHRISTIANS INTO THE FULL COMMUNION OF THE CATHOLIC CHURCH

All of you are one, united in Christ Jesus

387 This is the liturgical rite by which a person born and baptised in a separated ecclesial Community is received, according to the Latin rite,[1] into the full communion of the Catholic Church. The rite is so arranged that no greater burden than necessary (see Acts 15:28) is required for the establishment of communion and unity.[2] R1

388 In the case of Eastern Christians who enter into the fulness of Catholic communion, no liturgical rite is required, but simply a profession of Catholic faith, even if such persons are permitted, in virtue of recourse to the Apostolic See, to transfer to the Latin rite.[3] R2

389 In regard to the manner of celebrating the rite of reception: R3
    1. The rite should appear clearly as a celebration of the Church and have as its high point eucharistic communion. For this reason the rite should normally take place within Mass.
    2. Any appearance of triumphalism should be carefully avoided and the manner of celebrating this Mass should be decided beforehand and with a view to the particular circumstances. Both the ecumenical implications and the bond between the candidate and the parish community should be considered. Often it will be preferable to celebrate the Mass with only a few relatives and friends. If for a serious reason Mass cannot be celebrated, the reception should at least take place within a liturgy of the word, whenever this is possible. The person to be received into full communion should be consulted about the form of reception.

390 If the rite of reception is celebrated outside Mass, the Mass in which for the first time the newly received will take part with the Catholic community should be celebrated as soon as possible, in order to make clear the connection between the reception and eucharistic communion. R4

391 The baptised Christian is to receive both doctrinal and spiritual preparation, adapted to individual pastoral requirements, for reception into the full communion of the Catholic Church. The candidate should learn R5

---

[1] See Vatican Council II, Constitution on the Liturgy *Sacrosanctum Concilium*, art. 69, b; Decree on Ecumenism *Unitatis redintegratio*, no. 3. Secretariat for Christian Unity, *Ecumenical Directory I*, no. 19: AAS 59 (1967), 581.

[2] See Vatican Council II, Decree on Ecumenism *Unitatis redintegratio*, no. 18.

[3] See Vatican Council II, Decree on the Eastern Catholic Churches *Orientalium Ecclesiarum*, nos. 25 and 4.

to deepen an inner adherence to the Church, where he or she will find the fulness of his or her baptism. During the period of preparation the candidate may share in worship in conformity with the provisions of the *Ecumenical Directory.*

Anything that would equate candidates for reception with those who are catechumens is to be absolutely avoided.

392 One who was born and baptised outside the visible communion of the Catholic Church is not required to make an abjuration of heresy, but simply a profession of faith.[4]

393 The sacrament of baptism cannot be repeated and therefore it is not permitted to confer it again conditionally, unless there is a reasonable doubt about the fact or validity of the baptism already conferred. If serious investigation raises such prudent doubt and it seems necessary to confer baptism again conditionally, the minister should explain beforehand the reasons why this is being done and a nonsolemn form of baptism is to be used.[5]

The local Ordinary is to decide in each case what rites are to be included or excluded in conferring conditional baptism.

394 It is the office of the bishop to receive baptised Christians into the full communion of the Catholic Church. But a priest to whom the bishop entrusts the celebration of the rite has the faculty of confirming the candidate within the rite of reception,[6] unless the person received has already been validly confirmed.

395 If the profession of faith and reception take place within Mass, the candidate, according to his or her own conscience, should make a confession of sins beforehand, first informing the confessor that he or she is about to be received into full communion. Any confessor who is lawfully approved may hear the candidate's confession.

396 At the reception, the candidate should be accompanied by a sponsor and may even have two sponsors. If someone has had the principal part in guiding or preparing the candidate, he or she should be the sponsor.

397 In the eucharistic celebration within which reception into full communion takes place or, if the reception takes place outside Mass, in the Mass that follows at a later time, communion under both kinds is permitted for the person received, the sponsor, the parents and spouse who are Catholics, lay catechists who may have instructed the person, and, if the number involved and other circumstances make this feasible, for all Catholics present.

---

[4] See Secretariat for Christian Unity, *Ecumenical Directory I,* nos. 19 and 20: AAS 59 (1967), 581.

[5] See ibid., nos. 14-15: AAS 59 (1967), 580.

[6] See *Rite of Confirmation,* Introduction, no. 7, b.

398 The conferences of bishops may, in accord with the provisions of the R12 Constitution on the Liturgy, art. 63, adapt the rite of reception to various circumstances. The local Ordinary, by expanding or shortening the rite, may arrange it to suit the particular circumstances of the persons and place involved.[7]

399 The names of those received into the full communion of the Catholic R13 Church should be recorded in a special book, with the date and place of their baptism also noted.

---

[7] See Secretariat for Christian Unity, *Ecumenical Directory I*, no. 19: AAS 59 (1967), 581.

OUTLINE OF THE RITE

LITURGY OF THE WORD

Readings
Homily

CELEBRATION OF RECEPTION

Invitation
Profession of Faith
Act of Reception
[Confirmation]
    Laying on of Hands
    Anointing with Chrism
Celebrant's Sign of Welcome
General Intercessions
Sign of Peace

LITURGY OF THE EUCHARIST

RECEPTION WITHIN MASS

400 If the rite of reception into full communion takes place on R14 a solemnity or on a Sunday, the Mass of the day should be celebrated; on other days it is permissible to celebrate the Mass 'For the Unity of Christians' from the Masses for Various Needs.

LITURGY OF THE WORD

READINGS

401 The readings may be taken in whole or in part from those R14 provided in the Lectionary for Mass for the the day, for the rite of reception into full communion (Vol. III, pp. 74-85), or for the Mass 'For the Unity of Christians' (Vol. III, pp. 508-528), or from the Mass of Christian Initiation (Vol. III, pp. 18-47).

HOMILY

402 In the homily following the readings, the celebrant should R14 express gratitude to God for those being received and allude to their own baptism as the basis for their reception, to the sacrament of confirmation already received or about to be received, and to the eucharist, which for the first time they will celebrate with the Catholic community.

CELEBRATION OF RECEPTION

INVITATION

403 At the end of the homily, the celebrant in the following or R14 similar words invites the candidate to come forward with his or her sponsor and to make the profession of faith with the community. He may use these or similar words.

N., of your own free will you have asked to be received into the full communion of the Catholic Church. You have made your decision after careful thought under the guidance of the Holy Spirit. I now invite you to come forward with your sponsor and in the presence of this community to profess the Catholic faith. In this faith you will be one with us for the first time at the eucharistic table of the Lord Jesus, the sign of the Church's unity.

PROFESSION OF FAITH

404 The one to be received then joins the community in reciting the Nicene Creed, which is always said at this Mass.

The celebrant then asks the one to be received to add the following profession of faith. The candidate says:

I believe and profess all that the holy Catholic Church believes, teaches, and proclaims to be revealed by God.

ACT OF RECEPTION

405 The celebrant lays his right hand on the head of the candidate for reception and says the following. (The gesture is omitted when confirmation is to be conferred immediately.)

N., the Lord receives you into the Catholic Church.
His loving kindness has led you here,
so that in the unity of the Holy Spirit
you may have full communion with us
in the faith that you have professed in the presence of his family.

If confirmation is not celebrated, the celebrant's sign of welcome (no. 408) follows.

LAYING ON OF HANDS

406 If the person being received has not yet received the sacra- R17
ment of confirmation, the celebrant lays hands on the candidate's
head and begins the rite of confirmation with the following prayer.

All-powerful God, Father of our Lord Jesus Christ,
by water and the Holy Spirit
you freed your son/daughter from sin
and gave him/her new life.

Send your Holy Spirit upon him/her
to be his/her helper and guide.

Give him/her the spirit of wisdom and understanding,
the spirit of right judgment and courage,
the spirit of knowledge and reverence.
Fill him/her with the spirit of wonder and awe in your presence.

We ask this through Christ our Lord.

R. Amen.

ANOINTING WITH CHRISM

407 The sponsor places the right hand on the shoulder of the R17
candidate.

The celebrant dips his right thumb in the chrism and makes the
sign of the cross on the forehead of the one to be confirmed as
he says:

N., be sealed with the Gift of the Holy Spirit.

Newly confirmed:

Amen.

The celebrant adds:

Peace be with you.

Newly confirmed:

And also with you.

Celebrant's Sign of Welcome

408 The celebrant then takes the hands of the newly received person into his own as a sign of friendship and acceptance. With the permission of the Ordinary, another suitable gesture may be substituted, depending on local and other circumstances.

General Intercessions

409 In the introduction to the general intercessions the celebrant should mention baptism, (confirmation,) and the eucharist, and express gratitude to God. The one received into full communion is mentioned at the beginning of the intercessions. The celebrant may use these or similar words.

Brothers and sisters: our brother/sister N. has already been united to Christ through baptism [and confirmation] and now, with thanksgiving to God, we have received him/her into the full communion of the Catholic Church [and confirmed him/her with the gifts of the Holy Spirit]. Soon he/she will share with us at the table of the Lord. As we rejoice at the reception of a new member into the Catholic Church, let us join with him/her in asking for the grace and mercy of our Saviour.

Assisting minister:

For N., whom we have welcomed today as one of us, that he/she may have the help and guidance of the Holy Spirit to persevere faithfully in the choice he/she has made, we pray to the Lord:

R. Lord, hear our prayer.

Assisting minister:

For all who believe in Christ and for the Communities to which they belong, that they may come to perfect unity, we pray to the Lord:

R. Lord, hear our prayer.

Assisting minister:

For the Church [Communion] in which N. was baptised and received his/her formation as a Christian, that it may always grow in knowledge of Christ and proclaim him more effectively, we pray to the Lord:

R. Lord, hear our prayer.

Assisting minister:

For all in whom the spark of desire for God already burns, that they may be led to the fulness of truth in Christ, we pray to the Lord:

R. Lord, hear our prayer.

Assisting minister:

For those who do not yet believe in Christ the Lord, that they may enter the way of salvation by the light of the Holy Spirit, we pray to the Lord:

R. Lord, hear our prayer.

Assisting minister:

For all people, that they may be freed from hunger and war and live in peace and tranquillity, we pray to the Lord:

R. Lord, hear our prayer.

Assisting minister:

For ourselves, that as we have received the gift of faith, so too we may persevere in it to the end of our lives, we pray to the Lord:

R. Lord, hear our prayer.

The celebrant then says:

God our Father,
hear the prayers we offer
that we may continue our loving service to you.

Grant this through Christ our Lord.

R. Amen.

SIGN OF PEACE

410 After the general intercessions the sponsor and the entire assembly, if not too numerous, may greet the newly received person in a friendly manner. In this case the sign of peace before communion may be omitted. Finally, the one who has been received returns to his or her place.

R20

LITURGY OF THE EUCHARIST

411 Then the Mass continues. It is fitting that the person received and all those mentioned in no. 397 receive communion under both kinds.

RECEPTION OUTSIDE MASS

412 If, for a serious reason, the rite of reception into full communion takes place outside Mass, a liturgy of the word is to be celebrated.

R22

[If, in exceptional circumstances, not even a liturgy of the word is possible, just the celebration of reception itself takes place as described in nos. 403-410. It begins with introductory words in which the celebrant quotes from Scripture, for example, a text in praise of the mercy of God that has guided the candidate, and speaks of the eucharistic communion that will follow on the earliest day possible.]

R28

413 The celebrant, vested in alb, or at least surplice, with a stole of festive colour, greets those present.

R23

414 A suitable song may be sung, then there are one or more readings from Scripture, which the celebrant explains in the homily (see no. 402).

R24

The readings may be chosen from those provided in the Lectionary for Mass for the day, for the ritual Mass 'Christian Initiation apart from the Easter Vigil' (Vol. III, pp. 18-47), or for the Mass 'For the Unity of Christians' (Vol. III, pp. 508-528); but they are preferably chosen from those listed here, as indicated for the rite of reception into full communion (Vol. III, pp. 74-85).

NEW TESTAMENT READING (Lectionary, Vol. III, pp. 74-78)

1   Romans 8:28-39 — *He chose us specially to become true images of his Son.*

2   1 Corinthians 12:31 — 13:13 — *Love does not come to an end.*

3   Ephesians 1:3-14 — *God chose us in Christ to be holy and spotless through love.*

4   Ephesians 4:1-7, 11-13 — *There is one Lord, one faith, one baptism, and one God who is Father of all.*

5   Philippians 4:4-8 — *Fill your minds with everything that is pure.*

6   1 Thessalonians 5:16-24 — *May you all be kept blameless, spirit, soul and body, for the coming of our Lord Jesus Christ.*

RESPONSORIAL PSALM (Vol. III, pp. 78-81)

1   Psalm 26(27):1, 4, 8-9, 13-14
     R. (v.1a) **The Lord is my light and my help.**

2   Psalm 41(42):2-3; Psalm 43(44):3,4
     R. (Psalm 41[42]:3a) **My soul is thirsting for God, the God of my life.**

3   Psalm 60(61):2-6, 9
     R. (v.4a) **O Lord, you have been my refuge.**

4   Psalm 62(63):2-6, 8-9
     R. (v.3b) **For you my soul is thirsting, O Lord, my God.**
5   Psalm 64(65):2-6
     R. (v.2a) **To you our praise is due in Sion, O God.**
6   Psalm 120(121)
     R. (v.2a) **My help shall come from the Lord.**

GOSPEL (Vol. III, pp. 82-85)

1   Matthew 5:2-12a — *Rejoice and be glad, for your reward will be great in heaven.*
2   Matthew 5:13-16 — *Your light must shine in the sight of men.*
3   Matthew 11:25-30 — *You have hidden these things from the learned and the clever and revealed them to mere children.*
4   John 3:16-21 — *Everyone who believes in him will have eternal life.*
5   John 14:15-23, 26-27 — *We shall come to him and make our home with him.*
6   John 15:1-6 — *I am the vine, you are the branches.*

415 The reception itself, as given in nos. 402-408, follows.

416 Next there are intercessions, in the form given in no. 409 or in a similar form.

417 The rite is concluded as follows:

After the concluding prayer of the intercessions, the celebrant introduces the Lord's Prayer, in the following or similar words.

**Brothers and sisters,
let us join together and pray to God
as our Lord Jesus Christ taught us to pray:**

All:

Our Father . . .

If the person received was accustomed in his or her Community to the final doxology 'For the kingdom . . .,' it should be added here to the Lord's Prayer.

The celebrant gives the blessing in the usual manner. Then the sponsor and the entire assembly, if not too numerous, may offer to the newly received person some sign of welcome into the community. All then depart in peace.

Appendix 1
CELEBRATION AT THE EASTER VIGIL OF THE SACRAMENTS OF INITIATION AND OF THE RITE OF RECEPTION INTO THE FULL COMMUNION OF THE CATHOLIC CHURCH

The Father chose us in Christ to be holy and spotless in love

APPENDIX 1
CELEBRATION AT THE EASTER VIGIL OF THE SACRAMENTS OF INITIATION AND OF THE RITE OF RECEPTION INTO THE FULL COMMUNION OF THE CATHOLIC CHURCH

418 Pastoral considerations may suggest that along with the celebration of the sacraments of Christian initiation the Easter Vigil should include the rite of reception of already baptised Christians into the full communion of the Catholic Church. But such a decision must be guided by the theological and pastoral directives proper to each rite. The model provided here simply arranges the ritual elements belonging to such a combined celebration. But the model can only be used properly in the light of nos. 198-210, regarding celebration of the sacraments of Christian initiation, and of nos. 387-399, regarding the rite of reception into the full communion of the Catholic Church.

419 Inclusion at the Easter Vigil of the rite of reception into full communion may also be opportune liturgically, especially when the candidates have undergone a lengthy period of spiritual formation coinciding with Lent. In the liturgical year the Easter Vigil, the preeminent commemoration of Christ's paschal mystery, is the preferred occasion for the celebration in which the elect will enter the paschal mystery through baptism, confirmation, and eucharist. Candidates for reception, who in baptism have already been justified by faith and incorporated into Christ,[1] are entering fully into a community that is constituted by its communion both in faith and in the sacramental sharing of the paschal mystery. The celebration of their reception at the Easter Vigil provides the candidates with a privileged opportunity to recall and reaffirm their own baptism, 'the sacramental bond of unity [and] foundation of communion between all Christians.'[2] At the Easter Vigil these candidates can make their profession of faith by joining the community in the renewal of the baptismal promises, and, if they have not yet been confirmed, they can receive the sacrament of confirmation,

---

[1] See Secretariat for Christian Unity, *Ecumenical Directory I*, no. 11: AAS 59 (1967), 578-579 Vatican Council II, Decree on Ecumenism *Unitatis redintegratio*, no. 3.

[2] See *Ecumenical Directory I*, no. 11: AAS 59 (1967), 578. Vatican Council II, Decree on Ecumenism *Unitatis redintegratio*, no. 22.

which is intimately connected with baptism. Since of its nature baptism points to complete entrance into eucharistic communion,[3] the baptismal themes of the Easter Vigil can serve to emphasize why the high point of the candidates' reception is their sharing in the eucharist with the Catholic community for the first time (see no. 389,1).

420 The decision to combine the two celebrations at the Easter Vigil must be guided by the provision in the *Rite of Reception*, Introduction (no. 389,2). The decision should, then, be consistent in the actual situation with respect for ecumenical values and be guided by attentiveness both to local conditions and to personal and family preferences. The person to be received should always be consulted about the form of reception (see no. 389,2).

421 In its actual arrangement the celebration itself must reflect the status of candidates for reception into the full communion of the Catholic Church: such candidates have already been incorporated into Christ in baptism and anything that would equate them with catechumens is to be absolutely avoided (see no. 391).

---

[3] See Vatican Council II, Decree on Ecumenism *Unitatis redintegratio*, no. 22.

OUTLINE OF THE RITE

SERVICE OF LIGHT

LITURGY OF THE WORD

CELEBRATION OF BAPTISM

Presentation of the Candidates for Baptism
Invitation to Prayer
Litany of the Saints
Blessing of the Water
Profession of Faith
　　Renunciation of Sin
　　[Anointing with the Oil of Catechumens]
　　Profession of Faith
Baptism
Explanatory Rites
　　[Anointing after Baptism]
　　[Clothing with a Baptismal Garment]
　　Presentation of a Lighted Candle

RENEWAL OF BAPTISMAL PROMISES

Invitation
Renewal of Baptismal Promises
　　Renunciation of Sin
　　Profession of Faith
Sprinkling with Baptismal Water

CELEBRATION OF RECEPTION

Invitation
Profession by the Candidates
Act of Reception

CELEBRATION OF CONFIRMATION

Invitation
Laying on of Hands
Anointing with Chrism

LITURGY OF THE EUCHARIST

CELEBRATION AT THE EASTER VIGIL OF THE SACRAMENTS OF INITIATION AND OF THE RITE OF RECEPTION INTO THE FULL COMMUNION OF THE CATHOLIC CHURCH

422 Those who will be received into full communion at the Easter Vigil, along with their sponsors, should take places apart from the elect who will be called forward for the celebration of baptism.

The homily should include reference not only to the sacraments of initiation but also to reception into full communion (see no. 402).

CELEBRATION OF BAPTISM

423 The celebration of baptism begins after the homily. It takes place at the baptismal font, if this is in view of the faithful; otherwise in the sanctuary, where a vessel of water for the rite should be prepared beforehand.

PRESENTATION OF THE CANDIDATES FOR BAPTISM

424 Accordingly, one of the following procedures, options A, B, or C, is chosen for the presentation of the candidates for baptism.

A   *When Baptism Is Celebrated Immediately at the Baptismal Font*
The celebrant accompanied by the assisting ministers goes directly to the font. An assisting deacon or other minister calls the candidates for baptism forward and their godparents present them. Then the candidates and the godparents take their place around the font in such a way as not to block the view of the assembly. The invitation to prayer (no. 425) and the Litany of the Saints (no. 426) follow.

[If there are a great many candidates, they and their godparents simply take their place around the font during the singing of the Litany of Saints.]

B   *When Baptism Is Celebrated after a Procession to the Font*
There may be a full procession to the baptismal font. In this case
an assisting deacon or other minister calls the candidates for baptism forward and their godparents present them.

[If there are a great many candidates, they and their godparents simply take their place in the procession].

The procession is formed in this order: a minister carries the
Easter candle at the head of the procession (unless, outside the
Easter Vigil, it already rests at the baptismal font), the candidates with their godparents come next, then the celebrant with
the assisting ministers. The Litany of the Saints (no. 426) is sung
during the procession. When the procession has reached the font,
the candidates and their godparents take their place around the
font in such a way as not to block the view of the assembly. The
invitation to prayer (no. 425) precedes the blessing of the water.

C   *When Baptism Is Celebrated in the Sanctuary*
An assisting deacon or other minister calls the candidates for
baptism forward and their godparents present them. The candidates and their godparents take their place before the celebrant
in the sanctuary in such a way as not to block the view of the
assembly. The invitation to prayer (no. 425) and the Litany of
the Saints (no. 426) follow.

[If there are a great many candidates, they and their godparents simply take their place in the sanctuary during the singing
of the Litany of the Saints.]

INVITATION TO PRAYER

425 The celebrant addresses the following or a similar invitation for the assembly to join in prayer for the candidates for
baptism.

Dear friends, let us pray to almighty God for our brothers and
sisters, N. and N., who are asking for baptism. He has called
them and brought them to this moment; may he grant them
light and strength to follow Christ with resolute hearts and to
profess the faith of the Church. May he give them the new life
of the Holy Spirit, whom we are about to call down on this water.

Litany of the Saints

426 The singing of the Litany of the Saints is led by cantors and may include, at the proper place, names of other saints (for example, the titular of the church, the patron saints of the place or of those to be baptised) or petitions suitable to the occasion.

Lord, have mercy	Lord, have mercy
Christ, have mercy	Christ, have mercy
Lord, have mercy	Lord, have mercy

Holy Mary, Mother of God	pray for us
Saint Michael	pray for us
Holy Angels of God	pray for us
Saint John the Baptist	pray for us
Saint Joseph	pray for us
Saint Peter and Saint Paul	pray for us
Saint Andrew	pray for us
Saint John	pray for us
Saint Mary Magdalene	pray for us
Saint Stephen	pray for us
Saint Ignatius	pray for us
Saint Lawrence	pray for us
Saint Perpetua and Saint Felicity	pray for us
Saint Agnes	pray for us
Saint Gregory	pray for us
Saint Augustine	pray for us
Saint Athanasius	pray for us
Saint Basil	pray for us
Saint Martin	pray for us
Saint Benedict	pray for us
Saint Francis and Saint Dominic	pray for us
Saint Francis Xavier	pray for us
Saint John Vianney	pray for us
Saint Catherine	pray for us
Saint Teresa	pray for us
All holy men and women	pray for us

Lord, be merciful	Lord, save your people
From all evil	Lord, save your people
From every sin	Lord, save your people
From everlasting death	Lord, save your people
By your coming as man	Lord, save your people

By your death and rising to new life	Lord, save your people
By your gift of the Holy Spirit	Lord, save your people
Be merciful to us sinners	Lord, hear our prayer
Give new life to these chosen ones by the grace of baptism	Lord, hear our prayer
Jesus, Son of the living God	Lord, hear our prayer
Christ, hear us	Christ, hear us
Lord Jesus, hear our prayer	Lord Jesus, hear our prayer

BLESSING OF THE WATER

427 After the Litany of the Saints, facing the font (or vessel) containing the water, the celebrant says the following (music, p. 126).

Father,
you give us grace through sacramental signs,
which tell us of the wonders of your unseen power.

In baptism we use your gift of water,
which you have made a rich symbol of the grace
you give us in this sacrament.

At the very dawn of creation
your Spirit breathed on the waters,
making them the wellspring of all holiness.

The waters of the great flood
you made a sign of the waters of baptism
that make an end of sin
and a new beginning of goodness.

Through the waters of the Red Sea
you led Israel out of slavery
to be an image of God's holy people,
set free from sin by baptism.

In the waters of the Jordan
your Son was baptised by John
and anointed with the Spirit.

Your Son willed that water and blood should flow from his side
as he hung upon the cross.

After his resurrection he told his disciples:
'Go out and teach all nations,
baptising them in the name of the Father, and of the Son,
   and of the Holy Spirit.'

Father,
look now with love upon your Church
and unseal for it the fountain of baptism.

By the power of the Holy Spirit
give to this water the grace of your Son,
so that in the sacrament of baptism
all those whom you have created in your likeness
may be cleansed from sin
and rise to a new birth of innocence
by water and the Holy Spirit.

> Before continuing, the celebrant pauses and touches the water
> with his right hand, or he may instead lower the Easter candle
> into the water once or three times, then hold it there for the re-
> mainder of the blessing.

We ask you, Father, with your Son
to send the Holy Spirit upon the waters of this font.
May all who are buried with Christ in the death of baptism
rise also with him to newness of life.

We ask this through Christ our Lord.

> All:

Amen.

> If the Easter candle has been held in the water, the celebrant
> then raises it and the people sing the following or another suita-
> ble acclamation.

Springs of water, bless the Lord.
Give him glory and praise for ever.

PROFESSION OF FAITH

> 428 After the blessing of the water, the celebrant continues with
> the profession of faith, which includes the renunciation of sin
> and the profession itself (between these there may be the
> anointing).

Renunciation of Sin

429 Using one of the following formularies, the celebrant questions all the elect together; or, after being informed of each candidate's name by the godparents, he may use the same formularies to question the candidates individually.

[If circumstances require, the conference of bishops may make the three formularies more specific and detailed, especially in regions where it is necessary for the candidates to reject superstitious and magical practises (see no. 72).]

A   Celebrant:

Do you reject sin so as to live in the freedom of God's children?

Candidates:

I do.

Celebrant:

**Do you reject the glamour of evil,
and refuse to be mastered by sin?**

Candidates:

I do.

Celebrant:

Do you reject Satan, father of sin and prince of darkness?

Candidates:

I do.

B   Celebrant:

**Do you reject Satan,
and all his works,
and all his empty promises?**

Candidates:

I do.

C   Celebrant:

Do you reject Satan?

Candidates:

I do.

Celebrant:

And all his works?

Candidates:

I do.

Celebrant:

And all his empty promises?

Candidates:

I do.

ANOINTING WITH THE OIL OF CATECHUMENS

430 Unless the conference of bishops has decided on its omission (see no. 33,7) or it has been anticipated as a preparation rite (nos. 190-194), the anointing with the oil of catechumens takes place between the renunciation and the profession of faith.

The celebrant says:

We anoint you with the oil of salvation
in the name of Christ our Saviour.
May he strengthen you with his power,
who lives and reigns for ever and ever.

Candidates:

Amen.

The celebrant anoints each candidate with the oil of catechumens on both hands, on the breast, or, if this seems desirable, on other parts of the body.

[If there are a great many candidates, additional priests or deacons may assist in the anointing.]

PROFESSION OF FAITH

431 Then the celebrant, informed again of each candidate's name by the godparents, questions each candidate individually. Each candidate is baptised immediately after his or her profession of faith.

[If there are a great many to be baptised, the profession of faith
may be made simultaneously either by all together or group by
group, then the baptism of each candidate follows.]

Celebrant:

N., do you believe in God, the Father almighty,
   creator of heaven and earth?

Candidate:

I do.

Celebrant:

Do you believe in Jesus Christ, his only Son, our Lord,
   who was born of the Virgin Mary,
   was crucified, died, and was buried,
   rose from the dead,
   and is now seated at the right hand of the Father?

Candidate:

I do.

Celebrant:

Do you believe in the Holy Spirit,
   the holy catholic Church, the communion of saints,
   the forgiveness of sins, the resurrection of the body,
   and the life everlasting?

Candidate:

I do.

BAPTISM

432 The celebrant baptises each candidate either by immersion,
option A, or by the pouring of water, option B. Each baptism
may be followed by a short acclamation (Appendix, no. 452),
sung or said by the people.

[If there are a great number to be baptised, they may be divided
into groups and baptised by assisting priests or deacons. In baptising, either by immersion, option A, or by the pouring of water, option B, these ministers say the sacramental formulary for
each candidate. During the baptisms, singing by the people is
desirable or readings from Scripture or simply silent prayer.]

A   If baptism is by immersion, of the whole body or of the head only, decency and decorum should be preserved. Either or both godparents touch the candidate. The celebrant, immersing the candidate's whole body or head three times, baptises the candidate in the name of the Trinity.

N., I baptise you in the name of the Father,

He immerses the candidate the first time.

and of the Son,

He immerses the candidate the second time.

and of the Holy Spirit.

He immerses the candidate the third time.

B   If baptism is by the pouring of water, either or both godparents place the right hand on the shoulder of the candidate, and the celebrant, taking baptismal water and pouring it three times on the candidate's bowed head, baptises the candidate in the name of the Trinity.

N., I baptise you in the name of the Father,

He pours water the first time.

and of the Son,

He pours water the second time.

and of the Holy Spirit.

He pours water the third time.

EXPLANATORY RITES

433 The celebration of baptism continues with the explanatory rites, after which the celebration of confirmation normally follows.

ANOINTING AFTER BAPTISM

434 If the confirmation of those baptised is separated from their baptism, the celebrant anoints them with chrism immediately after baptism.

[When a great number have been baptised, assisting priests or deacons may help with the anointing.]

The celebrant first says the following over all the newly baptised before the anointing.

The God of power and Father of our Lord Jesus Christ
has freed you from sin
and brought you to new life
through water and the Holy Spirit.

He now anoints you with the chrism of salvation,
so that, united with his people,
you may remain for ever a member of Christ
who is Priest, Prophet, and King.

Newly baptised:

Amen.

In silence each of the newly baptised is anointed with chrism on the crown of the head.

Clothing with a Baptismal Garment

435 The garment used in this rite may be white or of a colour that conforms to local custom. If circumstances suggest, this rite may be omitted.

The celebrant says the following formulary, and at the words 'Receive this baptismal garment' the godparents place the garment on the newly baptised.

N. and N., you have become a new creation
and have clothed yourselves in Christ.
Receive this baptismal garment
and bring it unstained to the judgment seat
  of our Lord Jesus Christ,
so that you may have everlasting life.

Newly baptised:

Amen.

PRESENTATION OF A LIGHTED CANDLE

436 The celebrant takes the Easter candle in his hands or touches it, saying:

Godparents, please come forward to give to the newly baptised the light of Christ.

A godparent of each of the newly baptised goes to the celebrant, lights a candle from the Easter candle, then presents it to the newly baptised.

Then the celebrant says to the newly baptised:

You have been enlightened by Christ.
Walk always as children of the light
and keep the flame of faith alive in your hearts.
When the Lord comes, may you go out to meet him
with all the saints in the heavenly kingdom.

Newly baptised:

Amen.

RENEWAL OF BAPTISMAL PROMISES

INVITATION

437 After the celebration of baptism, the celebrant addresses the community, in order to invite those present to the renewal of their baptismal promises; the candidates for reception into full communion join the rest of the community in this renunciation of sin and profession of faith. All stand and hold lighted candles. The celebrant may use the following or similar words.

Dear friends,
through the paschal mystery
we have been buried with Christ in baptism,
so that we may rise with him to newness of life.
Now that we have completed our Lenten observance,
let us renew the promises we made in baptism,
when we rejected Satan and his works
and promised to serve God faithfully in his holy catholic Church.

RENEWAL OF BAPTISMAL PROMISES

RENUNCIATION OF SIN

438 The celebrant continues with one of the following formularies of renunciation.

[If circumstances require, the conference of bishops may adapt formulary A in accord with local conditions.]

A Celebrant:

Do you reject sin so as to live in the freedom of God's children?

All:

I do.

Celebrant:

**Do you reject the glamour of evil,
and refuse to be mastered by sin?**

All:

I do.

Celebrant:

Do you reject Satan, father of sin and prince of darkness?

All:

I do.

B Celebrant:

Do you reject Satan?

All:

I do.

Celebrant:

And all his works?

All:

I do.

Celebrant:

And all his empty promises?

All:

I do.

Profession of Faith

439 Then the celebrant continues:

Do you believe in God, the Father almighty,
  creator of heaven and earth?

All:

I do.

Celebrant:

Do you believe in Jesus Christ, his only Son, our Lord,
  who was born of the Virgin Mary,
  was crucified, died, and was buried,
  rose from the dead,
  and is now seated at the right hand of the Father?

All:

I do.

Celebrant:

Do you believe in the Holy Spirit,
  the holy catholic Church, the communion of saints,
  the forgiveness of sins, the resurrection of the body,
  and the life everlasting?

All:

I do.

Sprinkling with Baptismal Water

440 The celebrant sprinkles all the people with the blessed baptismal water, while all sing the following song or any other that is baptismal in character.

I saw water flowing
from the right side of the temple, alleluia.
It brought God's life and his salvation,
and the people sang in joyful praise:
alleluia, alleluia. (See Ezekiel 47:1-2,9)

The celebrant then concludes with the following prayer.

God, the all-powerful Father of our Lord Jesus Christ,
has given us a new birth by water and the Holy Spirit
and forgiven all our sins.
May he also keep us faithful to our Lord Jesus Christ
for ever and ever.

All:

Amen.

CELEBRATION OF RECEPTION

INVITATION

441 If baptism has been celebrated at the font, the celebrant,
the assisting ministers, and the newly baptised with their godparents proceed to the sanctuary. As they do so the assembly
may sing a suitable song.

Then in the following or similar words the celebrant invites the
candidates for reception, along with their sponsors, to come into
the sanctuary and before the community to make a profession
of faith.

N. and N., of your own free will you have asked to be received
into the full communion of the Catholic Church. You have made
your decision after careful thought under the guidance of the
Holy Spirit. I now invite you to come forward with your sponsors and in the presence of this community to profess the Catholic faith. In this faith you will be one with us for the first time
at the eucharistic table of the Lord Jesus, the sign of the Church's
unity.

PROFESSION BY THE CANDIDATES

442 When the candidates for reception and their sponsors have
taken their places in the sanctuary, the celebrant asks the candidates to make the following profession of faith. The candidates
say:

I believe and profess all that the holy Catholic Church believes,
teaches, and proclaims to be revealed by God.

443 Then the candidates with their sponsors go individually to the celebrant, who says to each candidate (laying his right hand on the head of any candidate who is not to receive confirmation):

N., the Lord receives you into the Catholic Church.
His loving kindness has led you here,
so that in the unity of the Holy Spirit
you may have full communion with us
in the faith that you have professed in the presence of his family.

CELEBRATION OF CONFIRMATION

444 Before the celebration of confirmation begins, the assembly may sing a suitable song.

445 If the bishop has conferred baptism, he should now also confer confirmation. If the bishop is not present, the priest who conferred baptism and received the candidates into full communion is authorized to confirm.

[When there are a great many persons to be confirmed, the minister of confirmation may associate priests with himself as ministers of the sacrament (see no. 14).]

INVITATION

446 The newly baptised with their godparents and, if they have not received the sacrament of confirmation, the newly received with their sponsors, stand before the celebrant. He first speaks briefly to the newly baptised and the newly received in these or similar words.

My dear candidates for confirmation, by your baptism you have been born again in Christ and you have become members of Christ and of his priestly people. Now you are to share in the outpouring of the Holy Spirit among us, the Spirit sent by the Lord upon his apostles at Pentecost and given by them and their successors to the baptised.

The promised strength of the Holy Spirit, which you are to receive, will make you more like Christ and help you to be witnesses to his suffering, death, and resurrection. It will strengthen you to be active members of the Church and to build up the Body of Christ in faith and love.

[The priests who will be associated with the celebrant as ministers of the sacrament now stand next to him.]

With hands joined, the celebrant next addresses the people:

My dear friends, let us pray to God our Father, that he will pour out the Holy Spirit on these candidates for confirmation to strengthen them with his gifts and anoint them to be more like Christ, the Son of God.

All pray briefly in silence.

Laying on of Hands

447 The celebrant holds his hands outstretched over the entire group of those to be confirmed and says the following prayer.

[In silence the priests associated as ministers of the sacrament also hold their hands outstretched over the candidates.]

All-powerful God, Father of our Lord Jesus Christ,
by water and the Holy Spirit
you freed your sons and daughters from sin
and gave them new life.

Send your Holy Spirit upon them
to be their helper and guide.

Give them the spirit of wisdom and understanding,
the spirit of right judgment and courage,
the spirit of knowledge and reverence.
Fill them with the spirit of wonder and awe in your presence.

We ask this through Christ our Lord.

R. **Amen.**

Anointing with Chrism

448 A minister brings the chrism to the celebrant.

[When the celebrant is the bishop, priests who are associated as ministers of the sacrament receive the chrism from him.]

Each candidate, with godparent or godparents or with sponsors, goes to the celebrant (or to an associated minister of the sacrament); or, if circumstances require, the celebrant (associated ministers) may go to the candidates.

Either or both godparents and sponsors place the right hand on the shoulder of the candidate; a godparent or a sponsor or the candidate gives the candidate's name to the minister of the sacrament. During the conferral of the sacrament an appropriate song may be sung.

The minister of the sacrament dips his right thumb in the chrism and makes the sign of the cross on the forehead of the one to be confirmed as he says:

N., be sealed with the Gift of the Holy Spirit.

Newly confirmed:

Amen.

The minister of the sacrament adds:

Peace be with you.

Newly confirmed:

And also with you.

After all have received the sacrament, the newly confirmed as well as the godparents and sponsors are led to their places in the assembly.

LITURGY OF THE EUCHARIST

449 Since the profession of faith is not said, the general intercessions begin immediately and for the first time the neophytes take part in them. Some of the neophytes also take part in the procession to the altar with the gifts.

450 With Eucharistic Prayers I, II, or III the special interpolations given in the Roman Missal, the ritual Mass, 'Christian Initiation: Baptism' are used.

451 It is most desirable that the neophytes and newly received, together with their godparents, sponsors, parents, spouses, and catechists, receive communion under both kinds.

Before saying 'This is the Lamb of God,' the celebrant may briefly remind the neophytes of the preeminence of the eucharist, which is the climax of their initiation and the centre of the whole Christian life. He may also mention that for those received into full communion this first full sharing with the Catholic community in eucharistic communion is the high point of their reception.

APPENDIX 2
ACCLAMATIONS, HYMNS, AND SONGS

Praised be the Father of our Lord Jesus Christ,
a God so merciful and kind

ACCLAMATIONS FROM SACRED SCRIPTURE

452 The following are acclamations from Sacred Scripture.

1　Lord God, who is your equal?
Strong, majestic, and holy!
Worthy of praise, worker of wonders! (Exodus 15:11)

2　God is light: in him there is no darkness. (1 John 1:5)

3　God is love; those who live in love, live in God. (1 John 4:16)

4　There is one God, one Father of all;
he is over all, and through all;
he lives in all of us. (Ephesians 4:6)

5　Come to him and receive his light! (Psalm 34:6)

6　Blessed be God who chose you in Christ. (See Ephesians 1:3-4)

7　You are God's work of art, created in Christ Jesus.
(Ephesians 2:10)

8　You are now God's children, my dearest friends.
What you shall be in his glory has not yet been revealed.
(1 John 3:2)

9　Think of how God loves you!
He calls you his own children,
and that is what you are. (1 John 3:1)

10　Happy are those who have washed their robes clean,
washed in the blood of the Lamb! (Apocalypse 22:14)

11　All of you are one,
united in Christ Jesus. (Galatians 3:28)

12　Imitate God; walk in his love,
just as Christ loves us. (Ephesians 5:1-2)

HYMNS IN THE STYLE OF
THE NEW TESTAMENT

453 The following are hymns in the style of the New Testament.

1   Praised be the Father of our Lord Jesus Christ,
a God so merciful and kind!
He has given us a new birth, a living hope,
by raising Jesus his Son from death.
Salvation is our undying inheritance,
preserved for us in heaven,
salvation at the end of time. (1 Peter 1:3-5)

2   How great the sign of God's love for us,
Jesus Christ our Lord:
promised before all time began,
revealed in these last days.
He lived and suffered and died for us,
but the Spirit raised him to life.
People everywhere have heard his message
and placed their faith in him.
What wonderful blessings he gives his people;
living in the Father's glory,
he fills all creation
and guides it to perfection. (See 1 Timothy 3:16)

SONGS FROM ANCIENT LITURGIES

454 The following are songs from ancient liturgies.

1   We believe in you, Lord Jesus Christ.
Fill our hearts with your radiance
and make us the children of light!

2   We come to you, Lord Jesus.
Fill us with your life.
Make us children of the Father
and one in you.

3   Lord Jesus, from your wounded side
       flowed streams of cleansing water;
       the world was washed of all its sin,
       all life made new again!

4   The Father's voice calls us above the waters,
       the glory of the Son shines on us,
       the love of the Spirit fills us with life.

5   Holy Church of God, stretch out your hand
       and welcome your children,
       new-born of water
       and of the Spirit of God.

6   Rejoice, you newly baptised,
       chosen members of the Kingdom.
       Buried with Christ in death,
       you are reborn in him by faith.

7   This is the fountain of life that floods the entire world,
       the water that took its beginning
       from the pierced side of Christ.
       You who are born again of this water,
       place your hope in the kingdom of heaven.

Appendix 3
Gospel Readings
for the Celebration of
Christian Initiation
of a Person
in Danger of Death

What is born of the flesh is flesh;
what is born of the Spirit is spirit.

GOSPEL READINGS FOR THE CELEBRATION OF CHRISTIAN INITIATION OF A PERSON IN DANGER OF DEATH

455 For pastoral convenience the gospel readings suggested in no. 355 are presented here in full.

1 A reading from the holy Gospel
according to Matthew   22:35-40

This is the greatest and the first commandment.

To disconcert Jesus, one of the Pharisees, a lawyer, put a question, 'Master, which is the greatest commandment of the Law?' Jesus said, 'You must love the Lord your God with all your heart, with all your soul, and with all your mind. This is the greatest and the first commandment. The second resembles it. You must love your neighbour as yourself. On these two commandments hang the whole Law, and the Prophets also.'

This is the Gospel of the Lord.

2 A reading from the holy Gospel
according to Matthew   28:18-20

Make disciples of all the nations; baptise them in the name of the Father and of the Son and of the Holy Spirit.

Jesus came up and spoke to his disciples. He said, 'All authority in heaven and on earth has been given to me. Go, therefore, make disciples of all the nations; baptise them in the name of the Father and of the Son and of the Holy Spirit, and teach them to observe all the commands I gave you. And know that I am with you always; yes to the end of time.'

This is the Gospel of the Lord.

3   A reading from the holy Gospel
     according to Mark   1:9-11

He was baptised in the Jordan by John.

Jesus came from Nazareth in Galilee and was baptised in the
Jordan by John. No sooner had he come up out of the water
than he saw the heavens torn apart and the Spirit, like a dove,
descending on him. And a voice came from heaven, 'You are
my Son, the Beloved; my favour rests on you.'

This is the Gospel of the Lord.

4   A reading from the holy Gospel according to John   3:1-6

Unless a man is born from above, he cannot see the kingdom of heaven.

There was one of the Pharisees called Nicodemus, a leading
Jew, who came to Jesus by night and said, 'Rabbi, we know
that you are a teacher who comes from God; for no one could
perform the signs that you do unless God were with him'. Jesus
answered:

'I tell you most solemnly,
unless a man is born from above,
he cannot see the kingdom of God.'

Nicodemus said, 'How can a grown man be born? Can he go
back into his mother's womb and be born again?' Jesus replied:

'I tell you most solemnly,
unless a man is born through water and the Spirit,
he cannot enter the kingdom of God:
what is born of the flesh is flesh;
what is born of the Spirit is spirit.'

This is the Gospel of the Lord.

5   A reading from the holy Gospel according to John   6:44-47

Everybody who believes has eternal life.

Jesus said to the crowd,

> 'No one can come to me
> unless he is drawn by the Father who sent me,
> and I will raise him up at the last day.
> It is written in the prophets:
> They will all be taught by God,
> and to hear the teaching of the Father,
> and learn from it,
> is to come to me.
> Not that anybody has seen the Father,
> except the one who comes from God:
> he has seen the Father.
> I tell you most solemnly,
> everybody who believes has eternal life.'

This is the Gospel of the Lord.